Frommer's

Washington, D.C.

day BY day®

4th Edition

by Meredith Pratt

FrommerMedia LLC

Contents

12 Favorite Moments   1

1 The Best Full-Day Tours   7
The Best of D.C. in 1 Day   8
The Best of D.C. in 2 Days   14
The Best of D.C. in 3 Days   20

2 The Best Special-Interest Tours   25
Political Washington   26
D.C. for Architecture Lovers   34
Washington for Kids   42
Historic Washington   48

3 The Best Museums   57
National Air & Space Museum   58
Musuem of Natural History   62
Musuem of American History   66
19th- & 20th-Century Art Museums   70
Special-Interest Museums   74

4 The Best Neighborhood Walks   77
Adams Morgan   78
U Street Corridor/14th Street   80
Dupont Circle   84
Georgetown   88
Penn Quarter   92
Capitol Hill   96

5 The Best Shopping   101
Shopping Best Bets   102
Shopping A to Z   106

6 The Best Outdoor Activities 113
Rock Creek Park   114
C&O Canal   118
Georgetown   122
The Mall & Tidal Basin   124

7 The Best Dining 127
Dining Best Bets   132
Restaurants A to Z   133

8 The Best Nightlife 143
Nightlife Best Bets   146
Nightlife A to Z   147

9 The Best Arts & Entertainment 153
Arts & Entertainment Best Bets   156
Arts & Entertainment A to Z   157

10 The Best Hotels 159
Hotel Best Bets   162
Hotels A to Z   163

The Savvy Traveler 169
Before You Go   170
Useful Numbers & Websites   170
Getting There   171
Getting Around   174
Fast Facts   177

Index 181

Published by:

Frommer Media LLC

ISBN: 978-1-62887-306-1 (print); 978-1-62887-307-8 (ebk)

Editorial Director: Pauline Frommer
Editor: Christine Ryan
Production Editor: Lindsay Conner
Photo Editor: Meghan Lamb
Cartographer: Roberta Stockwell
Compositor: Heather Pope
Indexer: Maro RioFrancos

Front cover photos, left to right: Thomas Jefferson Memorial © Orhan Cam; Smithsonian Castle © Robert Lyle Bolton; Houses in Georgetown © Richard Cavalleri.

Back cover photo: U.S. Capitol © Orhan Cam.

For information on our other products and services, please go to Frommers.com.

Frommer's also publishes its books in a variety of electronic formats. Some content that appears in print may not be available in electronic formats.

Manufactured in China

5   4   3   2   1

About This Guide

Organizing your time. That's what this guide is all about.

Other guides give you long lists of things to see and do and then expect you to fit the pieces together. The Day by Day guides are different. These guides tell you the best of everything, and then they show you how to see it in the smartest, most time-efficient way. Our authors have designed detailed itineraries organized by time, neighborhood, or special interest. And each tour comes with a bulleted map that takes you from stop to stop.

Hoping to relive the glory days of Washington and Jefferson, visit the pandas at the National Zoo, or tour the Smithsonian Institution's free museums? Planning a walk through Georgetown, or dinner and drinks where you can rub shoulders with lawmakers and other D.C. celebrities? Whatever your interest or schedule, the Day by Days give you the smartest routes to follow. Not only do we take you to the top attractions, hotels, and restaurants, but we also help you access those special moments that locals get to experience—those "finds" that turn tourists into travelers.

The Day by Days are also your top choice if you're looking for one complete guide for all your travel needs. The best hotels and restaurants for every budget, the greatest shopping values, the wildest nightlife—it's all here.

Why should you trust our judgment? Because our authors personally visit each place they write about. They're an independent lot who say what they think and would never include places they wouldn't recommend to their best friends. They're also open to suggestions from readers. If you'd like to contact them, please send your comments our way at feedback@frommers.com, and we'll pass them on.

Enjoy your Day by Day guide—the most helpful travel companion you can buy. And have the trip of a lifetime.

About the Author

A Baltimore native and a Washingtonian for more than 10 years, **Meredith Pratt** is an avid traveler, writer, and art lover. Her work has profiled international travel locales, high-powered personalities, and top D.C. destinations. Pratt's writing has appeared in *USA Today, Executive Travel, Baltimore Magazine, WedMD Magazine,* and *Washington Flyer,* among other places.

An Additional Note

Please be advised that travel information is subject to change at any time—and this is especially true of prices. We therefore suggest that you write or call ahead for confirmation when making your travel plans. The authors, editors, and publisher cannot be held responsible for the experiences of readers while traveling. Your safety is important to us, however, so we encourage you to stay alert and be aware of your surroundings.

Star Ratings, Icons & Abbreviations

Every hotel, restaurant, and attraction listing in this guide has been ranked for quality, value, service, amenities, and special features using a **star-rating system.** Hotels, restaurants, attractions, shopping, and nightlife are rated on a scale of zero stars (recommended) to three stars (exceptional). In addition to the star-rating system, we also use a **kids icon** to point out the best bets for families. Within each tour, we recommend cafes, bars, or restaurants where you can take a break. Each of these stops appears in a shaded box marked with a coffee-cup-shaped bullet ☕.

The following **abbreviations** are used for credit cards:

AE	American Express	DISC	Discover	V	Visa
DC	Diners Club	MC	MasterCard		

Frommers.com

Frommer's travel resources don't end with this guide. Frommer's website, **www.frommers.com,** has travel information on more than 4,000 destinations. We update features regularly, giving you access to the most current trip-planning information and the best airfare, lodging, and car-rental bargains. You can also listen to podcasts, connect with other Frommers.com members through our active-reader forums, share your travel photos, read blogs from guidebook editors and fellow travelers, and much more.

A Note on Prices

In the "Take a Break" (☕) and "Best Bets" sections of this book, we have used a system of dollar signs to show a range of costs for 1 night in a hotel (the price of a double-occupancy room) or the cost of an entree at a restaurant. Use the following table to decipher the dollar signs:

Cost	Hotels	Restaurants
$	under $130	under $15
$$	$130–$200	$15–$30
$$$	$200–$300	$30–$40
$$$$	$300–$395	$40–$50
$$$$$	over $395	over $50

How to Contact Us

In researching this book, we discovered many wonderful places—hotels, restaurants, shops, and more. We're sure you'll find others. Please tell us about them, so we can share the information with your fellow travelers in upcoming editions. If you were disappointed with a recommendation, we'd love to know that, too. Please write to: Support@FrommerMedia.com

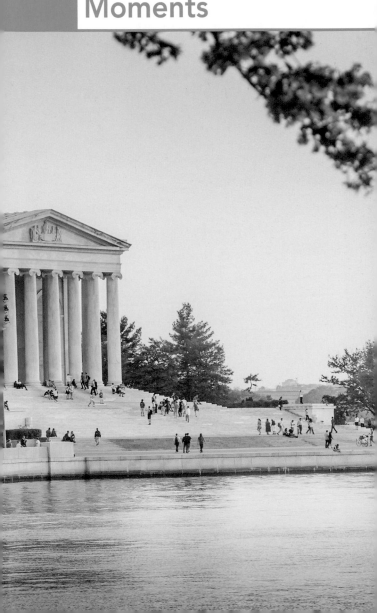

12 Favorite Moments

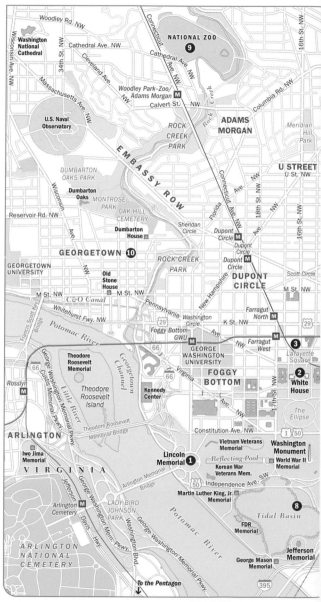

Woodley Rd. NW

Wisconsin Ave. NW

Washington National Cathedral

Cathedral Ave. NW

34th St. NW

Cleveland Ave

Massachusetts Ave. NW

Connecticut Ave. NW

NATIONAL ZOO
9

16th St. NW

U.S. Naval Observatory

ROCK CREEK PARK

Woodley Park-Zoo/ Adams Morgan **M**
Calvert St. NW

Rock Creek

ADAMS MORGAN

Columbia Rd. NW

Meridian Hill Park

EMBASSY ROW

DUMBARTON OAKS PARK

Wisconsin

Dumbarton Oaks

MONTROSE PARK

OAK HILL CEMETERY

Dumbarton House

Florida Ave. NW

18th St. NW

U STREET
U St. NW

16th St. NW

Reservoir Rd. NW

GEORGETOWN **10**

Sheridan Circle

Dupont Circle **M**

ROCK CREEK PARK

Dupont Circle

Dupont Circle **M**

DUPONT CIRCLE

Scott Circle

GEORGETOWN UNIVERSITY

Old Stone House

M St. NW

M St. NW

New Hampshire Ave.

M St. NW

C&O Canal

Whitehurst Fwy. NW

Pennsylvania Ave.

Washington Circle

Farragut North **M**

K St. NW

29

Francis Scott Key Bridge

Potomac River

Georgetown Channel

29

Foggy Bottom-GWU **M**

Farragut West **M**

3

Lafayette Square

7

Theodore Roosevelt Memorial

66

66

GEORGE WASHINGTON UNIVERSITY

Virginia Ave. NW

2
White House

Rosslyn **M**

Theodore Roosevelt Island

Kennedy Center

FOGGY BOTTOM

17th St. NW

The Ellipse

Theodore Roosevelt Memorial Bridge

ARLINGTON

George Washington Memorial Pkwy.

Little River

Constitution Ave. NW

1 50

Washington Monument

Iwo Jima Memorial

VIRGINIA

Vietnam Veterans Memorial

World War II Memorial

Lincoln Memorial **1**

Reflecting Pool

Korean War Veterans Mem.

Arlington Memorial Bridge

Jefferson Davis Hwy.

Arlington Cemetery **M**

George Washington Mem. Pkwy.

LADY BIRD JOHNSON PARK

Martin Luther King, Jr. Memorial

Independence Ave. SW

50

8

Tidal Basin

ARLINGTON NATIONAL CEMETERY

Washington Blvd.

Potomac River

George Washington Memorial Pkwy.

FDR Memorial

George Mason Memorial

Jefferson Memorial

To the Pentagon

395

Previous page: The Jefferson Memorial during cherry blossom season.

1 Lincoln Memorial

2 White House

3 Hay-Adams's Off the Record Bar

4 National Museum of American History

5 Eastern Market

6 Senate and House galleries at the U.S. Capitol Building

7 Ford's Theatre National Historic Site

8 Tidal Basin

9 National Zoological Park

10 Georgetown's mansions

11 National Gallery of Art

12 Dine out on 14th Street

President Harry Truman famously once said: "If you want a friend in Washington, get a dog." While it's true that the city is known for its passionate politics, presidential scandals, spies, and more, American politics, with its Hollywood-like allure, is not the only attraction drawing a never-ending stream of visitors to the nation's capital. It's a city of stunning architecture. World-class museums. Zeitgeist-changing theater. Cherry trees and great green spaces. Historic neighborhoods. Super shopping. An international pool of locals who call this place home. And, of course, the monuments that honor the brave, the fallen, and the founders of this fine country. Washington is inevitably targeted for laughs; but once you arrive in D.C., you'll be smiling, too.

❶ **Stand at the foot of the Lincoln Memorial and gaze across the National Mall.** The view—of the Reflecting Pool, the Vietnam and World War II memorials, the Washington Monument, and, in the distance, the Capitol Building—is monumental. See p 9.

❷ **Peer through the iron fence at 1600 Pennsylvania Avenue** for a glimpse of America's most famous residence. Unless you reserved a tour in advance, you can't get close, but the vision alone is enough to renew your patriotic spirit. See p 30.

❸ **Eavesdrop on the hushed conversations** between D.C. movers and shakers at the Hay-Adams' venerable Off the Record Bar. Then cross Lafayette Park, past the White House, to the POV Bar in the W Hotel for not-to-be missed views of the White House, National Mall, and Washington Monument. For more ideas on where you might run into the who's who of Washington over dinner or drinks, see the box "Where Politicos Drink & Dine" on p 24.

❹ **Marvel at the country's cultural and historic icons** at the Smithsonian's National Museum of American History. Sprawled across three floors, this museum houses everything from the only surviving

View of the Washington Monument from Constitution Gardens.

Indulge in tasty local treats or hunt for one-of-a-kind souvenirs at Eastern Market.

gunboat from the Revolutionary war to Julia Child's kitchen to the Star-Spangled Banner, the flag that was flying over Fort McHenry when the British attacked it in 1814, inspiring Francis Scott Key to write the poem that eventually became America's national anthem. See p 51.

⑤ Troll for treasures at Eastern Market on Capitol Hill. Savor a piping hot coffee and flaky pastry as you scavenge for secondhand baubles, retro clothing, colorful flowers, organic fruits and vegetables, and one-of-a-kind arts and crafts. See p 112.

⑥ Observe elected officials at work during a session of Congress. Or watch the American legal system in action, just a few blocks away, at the United States Supreme Court. See p 18.

⑦ Take in a show at Ford's Theatre. The historic site is a living memorial to President Abraham Lincoln, who was assassinated here by John Wilkes Booth in 1865. Along with an exhibit of collected artifacts including Booth's pistol and the President's clothing from the night he was shot, the theater hosts some of the most celebrated plays from Lincoln's period. See p 157.

⑧ Stroll along the Tidal Basin. This small reservoir adjacent to the Potomac River becomes a sea of blossoming pink flowers in March and April. Pose for a photo in front of the Jefferson Memorial or grab a paddle boat and hit the water in warmer months. See p 124.

⑨ Roar right along with the lions, tigers, and bears at the National Zoo. Then visit the famous giant pandas and expanded elephant house. And don't miss the petting zoo or the nearby "pizza" playground for very young children. See p 46.

The White House.

Think Pink

D.C. is another world in late March and April, when its ubiquitous Japanese cherry blossoms, a gift from the city of Tokyo in 1912, burst into bloom. Even politicians lose their pallor beneath the clouds of pink flowers along the Tidal Basin. The **National Cherry Blossom Festival** (☎ **877/44-BLOOM [442-5666];** www.nationalcherryblossomfestival.org) includes a kite festival, a dinner cruise, a Japanese street fair, and more.

⑩ **Bask in history amid George-town's massive mansions.** Most are at least 100 years old; many are older. In Georgian and Federal styles, they bear grand architectural details—such as round rooms and circular central staircases—that have all but disappeared from modern structures. See p 88.

⑪ **Wander the marble halls of The National Gallery of Art.** From Rothko to Rembrandt, the museum showcases some of the very best art and sculpture in the city. Take in traditional works in the West building then head to I.M. Pei's East Wing for more contemporary classics.

⑫ **Dine out along the 14th Street/U Street Corridor.** The energetic, regenerated neighborhood is surging with hip restaurants like Estadio, Le Diplomate or Provision No. 14. Choose one and you won't go wrong. See chapter 7 for dining recommendations. ●

The National Gallery of Art's striking, I.M. Pei-designed East Building.

1

The Best **Full-Day Tours**

The Best of D.C. in **1 Day**

1 Lincoln Memorial
2 Vietnam Veterans Memorial
3 Washington Monument
4 National World War II Memorial
5 Korean War Veterans Memorial
6 Martin Luther King, Jr. Memorial
7 FDR Memorial
8 Jefferson Memorial
9 PAUL
10 National Gallery of Art
11 National Museum of American History
12 The Source
13 Off the Record Bar

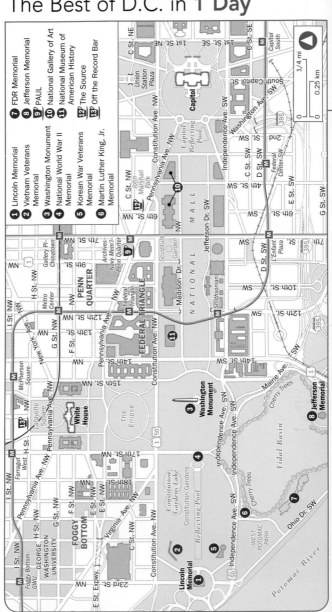

Previous Page: The U.S. Capitol building.

This full-day tour guides you through the Mall and Georgetown—both are must-sees, so don't let the fact that Georgetown is slightly off the public transportation grid deter you. These
two areas attract visitors in droves for good reason, so don't feel
like a lemming if you end up trailing kids in matching T-shirts as you
explore the Mall's free monuments and museums and then the
cobblestone sidewalks of M Street in Georgetown. START: **Metro to
Foggy Bottom, then a 30-minute walk.**

Biking past the Lincoln Memorial.

❶ ★★★ Lincoln Memorial.
Start your day on the steps of this
iconic tribute to Abraham Lincoln,
the beloved 16th president of the
United States. Architect Henry
Bacon designed this marble, Greek
temple–inspired memorial in 1914.
Its 36 Doric columns reflect the
states of the Union at the time of
Lincoln's assassination in 1865—
days after the Southern states sur-
rendered the Civil War. Daniel
Chester French designed the nearly
20-foot-tall (6m) sculpture of Lincoln, seated in solemn repose, surrounded by inscriptions of his
immortal words from the Gettys-
burg address and his second inaugural address. Gazing across The
Mall and contemplating Lincoln's
"dedication to the proposition that

all men are created equal" always
gives me chills. ⏱ *30 min.*
☎ *202/426-6841. www.nps.gov/linc.
Free admission. Metro: Foggy Bottom, then a 30-min. walk.*

**❷ ★★★ Vietnam Veterans
Memorial.** In Constitution Gardens, "The Wall" honors the 58,000
servicemen and -women who per-
ished or disappeared during the
Vietnam War. Two black slabs of
granite seem to grow from the
earth toward each other, rising in
height and joining to form a wide
"V." Designed in 1980 by Maya
Ying Lin, then an undergraduate at
Yale, it has been likened to a "scar
in the earth," evoking the deep rift
the war created among Americans.
The names of the dead and missing
are inscribed in the reflective stone.

Travel Tip

I recommend exploring D.C. on foot, but those who can't might consider **D.C. Tours** (☎ 212/852-4822; www.dctours.us). Its double decker sightseeing buses travel around the city and allow you to hop on and off at various stops. Buses leave every 15 and 30 minutes. One fare is good for the day ($49 for passengers 15 and up, $29 for kids 5–15, free under 5.). National Park Service rangers are on duty at the following monuments daily 9:30am–10pm. **Gray Line Buses** (☎ 202/779-9894; www.graylinedc.com) runs a loop from Union Station to the National Mall monuments and memorials. The cost is $30 per adult and $10 per child (3–11).

In reverent silence, mourning families make rubbings and leave flowers for their late sons, daughters, brothers, sisters, husbands, and wives. ⏱ *20 min.* ☎ *202/426-6841. www.nps.gov/vive. Free admission. Metro: Foggy Bottom, then a 25-min. walk.*

❸ **Washington Monument.** Robert Mills designed this 555-foot-tall (169m) monument to honor President George Washington. The world's tallest masonry structure when it was built in 1884, it's visible from points throughout the city. Its observatory and museum, accessible by an express elevator, offer breathtaking views of the capital city. ⏱ *20 min.* ☎ *202/426-6841. www.nps.gov/wamo. Free admission; tickets required for observation level. Metro: Smithsonian, then a 10-min. walk.*

❹ **National World War II Memorial.** After controversy between activists demanding a tribute to "the greatest generation" that fought and died in World War II, and naysayers who didn't want The Mall altered, this serene memorial was completed in 2004—without obstructing the views of the Lincoln Memorial or Washington Monument. Built of bronze and granite, it features 56 pillars that represent the unity of the states and territories in their decision to enter the war. The 4,000 sculpted gold stars on the Freedom Wall signify the 400,000 Americans who died fighting from 1941 to 1945. ⏱ *20 min.* ☎ *202/426-6841. www.nps.gov/nwwm. Free admission. Metro: Farragut West, Federal*

The Vietnam Veterans Memorial.

The Washington Monument towers over the National Mall.

Triangle, or Smithsonian, with a 25-min. walk.

⑤ Korean War Veterans Memorial. The representation of 19 larger-than-life ground soldiers slogging through a field, dressed in identical flowing rain capes, helmets, and battle gear, is haunting. Completed in 1986, it reminds viewers of a war forgotten by many, and honors the men and women who gave their lives for it. ⏱ *20 min.* ☎ *202/426-6841. www.nps. gov/kowa. Free admission. Metro: Foggy Bottom, then a 30-min. walk.*

⑥ Martin Luther King, Jr. Memorial. This monument, completed in August 2011, is a tribute to the Civil Rights leader who made his famous "I Have a Dream" speech on the steps of the Lincoln Memorial in 1963. A 30-foot-tall (9m) relief of King called the "Stone of Hope" is found just past two other pieces of granite known as the "Mountain of Despair," a visual metaphor for the struggles King encountered during his lifetime. ⏱ *20 minutes.* ☎ *202/426-6841. www.nps.gov/ mlkm. Free Admission. Metro: Smithsonian, then a 20-min. walk.*

⑦ FDR Memorial. This 7½-acre (3-hectare) outdoor memorial with four outdoor rooms, or galleries,

celebrates the man who saw the U.S. through the Great Depression and much of World War II. Designed by Lawrence Halprin in 1978 (and completed in 1997), it tells the story of Franklin Delano Roosevelt's four-term presidency: Each gallery represents the challenges of the time and showcases FDR's most famous quotes alongside sculptures of soup lines, the president in his wheelchair, his passionately political wife Eleanor, and more. ⏱ *20 min.* ☎ *202/426-6841. www.nps.gov/frde. Free admission. Metro: Smithsonian, then a 30-min. walk.*

⑧ ★★★ Jefferson Memorial. Modeled after the Pantheon in Rome, this circular colonnaded

The Korean War Veterans Memorial.

The Washington Skyline

As you wander among the monuments, memorials, and museums, you can't help but notice the **U.S. Capitol Building** (see p 28), at the eastern end of The Mall; the **Federal Reserve Building** on Constitution Avenue, almost directly across from the Vietnam Veterans Memorial; and the **White House,** behind its imposing wrought-iron fence, at 1600 Pennsylvania Ave. The **Capitol Visitors Center** (p 17) features an exhibit hall and detailed building tour information. The **White House Visitor Center,** at 15th Street and Pennsylvania Avenue, NW, offers details on the residence and a 14-minute video. See "Political Washington" on p 31 for more information.

structure fronts the picturesque Tidal Basin, which is lined with cherry trees that burst into rosy color from late March through mid-April. Architect John Russell drew from Thomas Jefferson's love of neoclassical design to celebrate the third president's contributions as a scientist, architect, politician, musician, diplomat, and inventor. Dedicated in 1943, it features a 19-foot-tall (5.7m) bronze statue of Jefferson inside. ⏱ *20 min.* ☎ *202/426-6841. www.nps.gov/ thje. Free admission. Metro: Smithsonian, then a 25-min. walk.*

The 30-foot tall relief of Dr. Martin Luther King, Jr. was completed in 2011.

9 **kids** **Paul.** It's tough to know where to find a quick bite to eat amid so many museums and government buildings. Just one block off the National Mall, this cafe has a solid menu of salads, sandwiches, quiche, espresso drinks, and baked goods. *801 Pennsylvania Ave., NW.* ☎ *202/524-4500. $. Metro: Archives.*

10 ★★★ **National Gallery of Art.** If you visit only one of the city's free art museums, make it this one. Founded in 1937, the museum has a permanent collection that spans 9 centuries of masterworks: early Italian and Flemish Renaissance paintings; the High Renaissance works of Titian; the Dutch interiors of Vermeer; the pre-Impressionist and Impressionist works of Monet, Manet, van Gogh, Degas, Toulouse-Lautrec, Gauguin, and Cézanne; and the modern masterpieces of Picasso, O'Keeffe, Johns, and Pollock, to name a few. Art lovers may want to clear out a whole day to wander these halls. Everyone else, allot 2 hours before heading to the National Museum of American History, your next stop. ⏱ *2 hr. See p 72 for service details.*

⓫ ★★ National Museum of American History. Want to see the original Kermit the Frog hand puppet? How about Dorothy's ruby red slippers, Archie Bunker's chair, or Muhammad Ali's boxing gloves? America's history is told through its objects, art, advertising, communications, and songs at this popular museum. The Star-Spangled Banner, the flag that inspired the national anthem, has been restored and is now housed in a dramatic new gallery and atrium dedicated to its preservation. Julia Child's kitchen, a 1903 Winton—the first car driven across the United States—and more than two dozen dresses from First Ladies including Laura Bush, Jackie Kennedy, and Michelle Obama are just a few more of the objects on display here. ⓘ *1 hr. See p 66.*

Statues, quotations and four outdoor galleries punctuate the sprawling grounds of the FDR Memorial.

⓬ ★★★ The Source. After touring The Mall, head just north to the Newseum, where you'll find this sleek, glass-walled restaurant owned by celebrity chef Wolfgang Puck. An American menu with an Asian twist features tuna tartare, lobster dumplings, Chinese duckling and American seafood and steak. *See p 142.*

⓭ ★★ Off the Record Bar. No visit to D.C. would be complete without a stop at this legendary drinking establishment in the historic Hay-Adams Hotel, across Lafayette Park from the White House. The bar is a favorite place to see and be seen in the District and a haunt of journalists, lobbyists, politicians, and statesmen—some of whom just might be pictured in the dozens of political caricatures on display. *See p 151.*

The National Gallery of Art's neoclassical West Building.

The Best of D.C. in **2 Days**

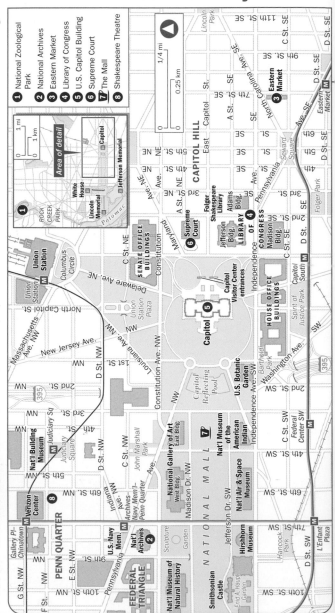

1 National Zoological Park
2 National Archives
3 Eastern Market
4 Library of Congress
5 U.S. Capitol Building
6 Supreme Court
7 The Mall
8 Shakespeare Theatre

Begin your second day at the National Zoo—home to giant pandas, lions, tigers, elephants, and other rare species. If you set out early enough (the zoo grounds open at 8am), you'll have time left to explore Capitol Hill—from the bustle of Eastern Market to the hustle of lawmakers and judges in the U.S. Capitol and Supreme Court buildings, both open for tours and spectators.
START: **Metro to Woodley Park–Zoo.**

❶ ★★★ 𝗸𝗶𝗱𝘀 **National Zoo-logical Park.** The giant pandas are the main attraction at this 163-acre (65 hectare) park in downtown D.C. You won't need tickets to catch a glimpse of any of the rare creatures here, but crowds regularly flock to see the pandas romp through their enclosure and eat frozen treats, so be sure to get there early if seeing the bears is a priority. Established in 1889, the National Zoo is home to some 500 species, many of them rare and/or endangered. You'll see cheetahs, zebras, gorillas, seals, monkeys, meerkats, and, of course, lions, tigers, and (other) bears. If you have very young children, the hilly terrain can be tiring, especially on hot days. The zoo rents strollers, and the Kids' Farm provides a nice break from all that walking; aimed at kids 3 to 8, the area lets little ones get an up-close look at ducks, chickens, goats, cows, and miniature donkeys. ⏱ *60–90 min. Allow 20 min.*

The gorilla exhibit at the National Zoo.

for Metro to next tour stop. 3001 Connecticut Ave. NW, adjacent to Rock Creek Park. ☎ *202/633-4888. www.nationalzoo.si.edu. Free admission. Daily Mar–Oct (weather permitting): grounds 8am–7pm; visitor center and animal buildings 9am–6pm. Daily Oct–Mar grounds 8am–5pm; visitor center and animal buildings 9am–4pm. Metro: Woodley Park–Zoo/Adams Morgan or Cleveland Park.*

See high-flying orangutans for free at the National Zoo.

Eating at the Zoo

Need a quick coffee or snack? Look for one of the eateries on zoo grounds: the Mane Grill on Lion/Tiger Hill, Panda Grill near the Giant Panda Habitat, or Seal Rock Café on the American Trail. Most eateries are seasonal and closed November to March, except for Mane Grill. Vending machines are positioned near restrooms and information facilities throughout the park.

❷ ★★ National Archives. After the Zoo, return to the Metro and head for the National Mall where you'll find, among the Smithsonian museums, some of the most important historic documents in U.S. history. The original Declaration of Independence, signed by members of Congress, the Constitution, the Bill of Rights, and other fascinating glimpses into America's past are on display in the Rotunda of the National Archives Building. You can also see the Emancipation Proclamation, Articles of Confederation, Edison's light bulb patent, and letters from Abraham Lincoln can also be ogled at this monument to history. ⏱ *1 hr. Hour-long guided tours are available Mon–Fri, 9:45am. Free admission. Reservations for timed visit entry are encouraged. 700 Pennsylvania Ave, NW. www.*

See some of the United States' founding documents at the National Archives Museum.

archives.gov/museum. Open daily 10am–5:30pm. Closed Thanksgiving and Dec 25. Metro: Archives/Navy Memorial.

❸ ★★ Eastern Market. Built in 1873, this city institution is a flea market, farmer's market, and crafts fair all rolled into one. Recharge over lattes, pancakes, muffins, omelets, or even ham sandwiches and salt-and-vinegar chips here before you shop. The outdoor lot fills on weekends (Mar–Dec) with farmers and fresh produce, artisans and ceramics, and bargain-hunters haggling over a mishmash of antiques. *See p 99 for service details.*

❹ Library of Congress. Want to see the original "rough draft" of the Declaration of Independence written in Thomas Jefferson's own hand? It's one of many American treasures here, along with the papers of other presidents, historic maps, revolving exhibitions, and multimedia resources. Created in 1800, the small library was burned by the British in 1814 during their infamous siege on Washington, but it was quickly re-established once Jefferson donated his personal collection of books and artifacts. Families with kids in tow can take a break from sightseeing and read some books together in the Young Readers Center (on the ground

The ornate interior of the Library of Congress.

floor of the Thomas Jefferson Building). The library also has a cafe, two snack bars, and a coffee shop. ⏱ *1 hr.; arrive 30 min. before tour begins. Docent-led, scheduled public tours depart Mon–Sat, in the Great Hall of the Thomas Jefferson Building, at 10:30, 11:30am, 12:30, 1:30, 2:30, and 3:30pm. No 3:30pm tour on Saturdays. Free admission. 1st St. SE (between Independence Ave. and E. Capitol St).* www.loc.gov. *Mon–Sat. 8:30am–5pm, except for federal holidays. Metro: Capitol South or Union Station.*

⑤ ★★★ U.S. Capitol Building. This majestic, 19th-century neoclassical landmark has served as the seat of American lawmaking since the first Congress in 1800. In 1793, George Washington laid the cornerstone of Dr. William Thornton's original design, and various architects saw to the building's completion in 1819. A museum of American art and history, as well as its principal civic forum, the Capitol is worth a stop just to see its architecture and hundreds of paintings, sculptures, and other artworks throughout its 17-acre (6.8-hectare) floor area. The exhibition hall of the Capitol Visitor Center features the original plaster cast of the *Statue of Freedom*, the bronze statue that stands atop the Capitol dome, as well as 24 sculptures from the Capitol's Statuary Hall depicting each state's favorite sons and daughters. All food, beverages, large bags, and pointed objects are prohibited. ⏱ *1 hr. Enter at the Capitol Visitors Center on E. Capitol St. at 1st St. NW. Mon–Sat 8:30am–4:30pm except Thanksgiving, Dec 25, and Jan 1. Free admission. Tours can be pre-booked online.* ☎ *202/226-8000.* www.visit thecapitol.gov. *Metro: Capitol South or Union Station.*

After dark, spotlights enhance the majestic beauty of Washington's monuments and buildings.

Stop in Union Station for a snack, or just to admire the architecture.

Travel Tip

You can find complete coverage of how to view the House or Senate galleries in session in "Political Washington" (see p 26).

6 ★★ **Supreme Court.** The chamber of the U.S. Supreme Court, the highest tribunal in the land, has been restored to its mid-19th-century appearance. Its nine justices, appointed for life terms, decide our collective fate—whether they're weighing in on federal laws or, more rarely, sealing a contested presidential election. The court convenes the first Monday in October and stays in session until it has heard all its cases and handed down decisions. The Court hears oral arguments the first 2 weeks of each month on Monday, Tuesday, and Wednesday. Visitors can listen to the arguments on short tours, or they can watch the day's entire proceedings. ⊕ 1–2 hr.; lines can be long, so be prepared to wait for up to 1 hr. If you're a legal eagle or Court TV fanatic and absolutely must see the day's full proceedings, arrive by 8:30am and get in line early, for first-come, first-served seating.

Everyone else can start at 2pm or 3pm and gain entry with time to spare. 1 1st St. NE (between E. Capitol St. and Maryland Ave. NE). ☎ 202/479-3211. www.supremecourtus.gov. Free admission. Mon–Fri 9am–4:30pm, except for federal holidays. Metro: Capitol South or Union Station.

7 **The Mall.** You have an hour or two before dinner and don't want to spoil it. If the weather is warm, grab a soda and snack at any of the many vendor carts stationed on The Mall. Then, either relax on the grass and people-watch, admire the sights, check out a monument, or take in one of the dozens of events held on The Mall through the year—from kite-flying festivals to international dance performances. (Visit www.nps.gov/mall for a schedule.) Otherwise, take shelter at Union Station (Columbus Circle at Massachusetts Ave. and 1st St., NE), just a few blocks north, where you'll find snacks, coffee, shopping, and stunning architecture—plus a Metro station for transportation to your next stop.

The imposing exterior of the U.S. Supreme Court building.

❽ ★★ The Shakespeare Theatre. Catch the Bard's best, from *A Midsummer's Night's Dream* to *Othello,* in productions with astounding sets and nationally known actors. Just steps from the Verizon Center, the company performs in the state-of-the-art Harman Center for the Arts. It has 2 stages (the 451-seat Lansburgh Theatre and the 774-seat Sydney Harman Hall), but there's not a bad seat in the house. The company's interpretations of Shakespeare's classics often feature a twist, such as an all-male cast or modern costumes (a recent production of Othello was set at the end of World War I, for example). The company also puts on plays by contemporaries of Shakespeare, such as Ben Johnson, as well as modern classics by such playwrights as Tennessee Williams, George Bernard Shaw, and Henrik Ibsen. *450 7th St. NW (between D and E sts.).* ☎ *202/547-1122. www.shakespearedc.org. Tickets $23–$68. Metro: Gallery Place/ Chinatown or Archives/Navy Memorial.*

The Best of D.C. in **3 Days**

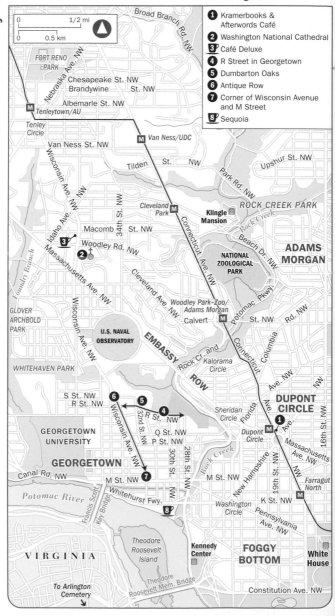

1 Kramerbooks & Afterwords Café

2 Washington National Cathedral

3 Café Deluxe

4 R Street in Georgetown

5 Dumbarton Oaks

6 Antique Row

7 Corner of Wisconsin Avenue and M Street

8 Sequoia

On your third day, leave the downtown crowds behind and explore Dupont Circle and the National Cathedral. Then spend a leisurely afternoon browsing, spending some dosh, and sipping espressos in Georgetown. By the end of Day 3, you'll feel as though you know Washington—and I bet you won't want to leave. START: **Metro to Dupont Circle.**

1 ★★ **Kramerbooks & Afterwords Café & Grill.** This bookstore, cafe, and coffee shop is the nerve center of Dupont Circle. A legendary gathering place, it's always packed with cool college kids, stylish gay men, voracious readers, debating politicians, and curious tourists who feel the urge to pick up Walt Whitman's Leaves of Grass. Open early in the morning and late at night, it's the perfect spot to start the day, over breakfast and the *Washington Post*. ⏱ *1 hr. 1517 Connecticut Ave. NW (between Dupont Circle and Q St.). Cafe* ☎ *202/387-3825. Bookstore* ☎ *202/387-1400. www.kramers. com. Breakfast $45–$17; lunch $13–$17; dinner $16–$25. Daily 7:30am–1am; Fridays and Saturdays until 4am. Metro: Dupont Circle.*

You can linger over the Washington Post with a cup of coffee at the legendary Kramerbooks.

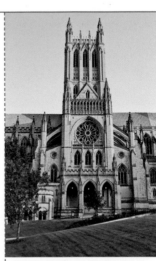

Washington National Cathedral.

2 ★★★ **Washington National Cathedral.** This glorious cathedral is where presidents are eulogized and sometimes interred, and where many a member of high society is wed. With vaulted ceilings and rich stone carvings, the English Gothic architecture incorporates stones from shrines and historic buildings around the universe—including outer space. That's right: A piece of lunar rock from the Apollo 11 mission is embedded in the stained-glass Space Window. It's a big hit with kids, as is the Darth Vader gargoyle hidden among the spires. The Episcopalian church has no local congregation; rather, it has functioned as a national house of prayer for various denominations, including Jewish and Serbian Orthodox citizens. Download your own self-guided tour at www.cath edral.org. ⏲ *1 hr. Start: 11am. Massachusetts and Wisconsin aves. NW.* ☎ *202/537-6200. Adults $11; Kids (5–17) $7; Kids under 5 Free. Free Sun and for other worship, prayer, and spiritual visits. Mon–Fri 10am–5:30pm; Sat 10am–4:30pm; Sun 8am–5pm. No direct Metro access.*

3 ★★ **kids** Café Deluxe. Airy and bright, this bustling neighborhood bistro serves New American classics such as roasted chicken, tuna steaks, and burgers. With small portions and crayons for kids, this is a favorite among families. ⏲ *1 hr. 3228 Wisconsin Ave. NW (at Macomb St.).* ☎ *202/686-2233. $. No direct Metro access.*

4 R Street in Georgetown. With its four- and five-story brick Federal and Georgian-style mansions; its private gardens rife with red tulips and pale pink hydrangeas; and its uniform row houses and manicured lawns, this street epitomizes residential Georgetown. Simply put, R Street between Wisconsin Avenue and 28th Street NW

Dumbarton Oaks, former home of Mildred and Robert Woods Bliss.

is where most Washingtonians would choose to live if money were no object. It is also home to a spectacular botanical garden, a historic park, meandering trails with romantic benches and weeping willow trees, and a grand, peaceful cemetery. ⏲ *2 hr.*

5 Dumbarton Oaks. Once a private residence, this 19th-century mansion is a research center for studies in Byzantine and pre-Columbian art and history, as well as landscape architecture. A former cow pasture, the grounds of Dumbarton Oaks were fashioned into staggeringly beautiful traditional European gardens, with an orangery, crocus, scilla, narcissus, magnolia, and cherry blossoms. Walkways are lined with bubbling fountains, stone archways, romantic hideaways, tiled pools, and a Roman-style amphitheater. The gardens remain open year-round (March 15–Oct 31 are peak months). ⏲ *30 min. 1703 32nd St. NW (garden entrance at 31st and R sts.).* ☎ *202/339-6401. www.doaks. org. Gardens: $10 adults; $8 seniors; $5 students and children (12 and under). Tues–Sun year-round; Mar 15–Oct 31 2–6pm, Nov 1–Mar 14 2–5pm (except national holidays and Dec 24). No Metro access.*

6 Antique Row. Depending on which way you're walking, Antique Row is either a cool cruise downhill or a steep uphill climb. In either case, antiques lovers won't care— they'll be too busy gaping at the storefronts with mint-condition 18th-century divans, beautifully painted Persian consoles, weathered ceramic water jugs, and all sorts of one-of-a-kind finds. The best of the lot: Carling Nichols, David Bell, and for early-20th-century fans, Random Harvest. Expect to pay top dollar. ⏲ *45 min. Wisconsin Ave., from S to N sts.*

Arlington National Cemetery

Arlington National Cemetery's 612 acres (248 hectares) honors national heroes and more than 400,000 war dead, veterans, and dependents. Many famous Arlington graves bear nothing more than simple markers, such as five-star General John J. Pershing's tomb. Highlights include the **Tomb of the Unknowns,** containing the unidentified remains of service members from World War I, World War II, and the Korean War. **Arlington House** (☎ **703/235-1530;** www.nps.gov/arho), built by Martha and George Washington's grandson, George Washington Parke Custis, is a 20-minute walk from the Visitor Center. **Pierre Charles L'Enfant's grave,** near Arlington House, is believed to afford the best view of Washington, the city he designed. Below Arlington House is the **gravesite of President John Fitzgerald Kennedy.** Jacqueline Kennedy Onassis rests next to her husband, and Robert Kennedy is buried close by. Arrive close to 8am if you want to contemplate the site in peace. The **Visitor Center** offers a detailed map and restrooms.

Tombstones at Arlington.

❼ ★★ Corner of Wisconsin Avenue and M Street. Look down M Street and you'll spy Intermix, Coach, Lacoste, Sephora, Wink, Madda Fella, Kate Spade, and the design district, Cady's Alley. Look up Wisconsin and see Benetton, Ralph Lauren, the Apple Store, Baby Gap, and a slew of antiques stores. It could be an expensive afternoon. When you're all shopped out, walk south,

Where Politicos Drink & Dine

★★ **The Monocle** (107 D St. NE; ☎ **202/546-4488**) is a favorite haunt among Members of Congress for its steak and seafood. Also on the Hill: **Tune Inn** (331 Pennsylvania Ave., SE; ☎ **202/543-2725**) and **Barrel** (613 Pennsylvania Ave. SE; ☎ **202/543-3622**). These bars are the perfect spots to eavesdrop on the scuttlebutt of young Hill staffers and Capitol Hill dwellers. In Penn Quarter, **The Capital Grille** (601 Pennsylvania Ave. NW; ☎ **202/737-6200**) is ground zero for cigars, Scotch, steaks, suspenders, and high-level lobbying. Look for the sideshow of 20-something interns duking it out with 40-something power mavens for the attentions of congressmen on the make. Catch prominent members of Congress wheeling and dealing at **Charlie Palmer Steak** (101 Constitution Ave., NW; ☎ **202/547-8100**), a tasty mainstay for lunchtime steaks and crab cakes. Steps from the White House, in the Hay-Adams Hotel, **Off the Record Bar** (800 16th St. NW; ☎ **202/942-7599**) serves stiff drinks to power-mongers. The very preppy **Smith Point** (1338 Wisconsin Ave. NW; ☎ **202/333-9003**) is the hotspot among SUV-driving Young Republicans. It's where to head for Nantucket-style entrees—and the latest looks in Lacoste wear.

downhill, on Wisconsin Avenue. It will deliver you to the Washington Harbor and the Potomac River.
🕐 *1½ hr. Metro to Tenleytown/AU, then take any 30 series bus (30S, 31, 32, or 37) going south on Wisconsin Ave.*

8 **Sequoia.** Stroll the promenade, gaze at the boats slicing through the Potomac waves, and then order a cocktail or cold beer at Sequoia—you deserve to sit down and relax. 🕐 *3000 K St. NW (waterfront).* ☎ *202/944-4200. Cocktails $7–$10. Lunch & dinner daily. Metro: Foggy Bottom.* ●

Political Washington

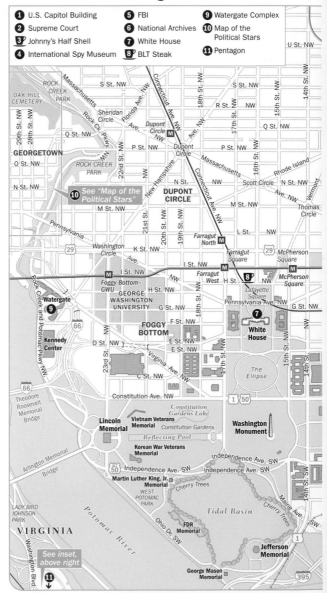

1. U.S. Capitol Building
2. Supreme Court
3. Johnny's Half Shell
4. International Spy Museum
5. FBI
6. National Archives
7. White House
8. BLT Steak
9. Watergate Complex
10. Map of the Political Stars
11. Pentagon

Previous page: View of the Lincoln Memorial, Washington Monument, and the Capitol Building.

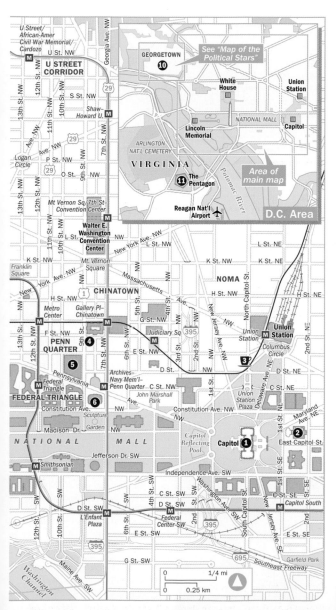

Oh, the intrigue . . . the drama . . . the repressed yawns among members of Congress as they fight to stay awake during marathon legislative sessions on Capitol Hill. Exciting or not, Washington is pure politics, 24/7. If you live here, there's no escape from the maneuverings of our elected officials, and the (sometimes biting, sometimes toothless) press corps that hounds them. If you're visiting, spend a few days catching a glimpse of the capital's complex, consequential, and at times truly captivating political scene, from past to present, with this tour. START: **Metro to Capitol South or Union Station.**

❶ ★★★ The U.S. Capitol Building.

Viewed from the wide avenues that radiate toward and away from it, the Capitol is almost palatial in its grandeur, crowning the highest pont between the Potomac and Anacostia rivers. Connected to the White House by a grand diagonal avenue (Pennsylvania Ave.), the Capitol was part of architect Pierre L'Enfant's plan to embody the separation of powers in the capital grid and architecture when he laid out the city in 1791. The Capitol complex includes the Capitol, the House and Senate Office buildings, the U.S. Botanic Garden, the Capitol Grounds, the Library of Congress buildings, and the Supreme Court building. Among the Capitol's most impressive features are the cast-iron dome, the rotunda, the old Senate and Supreme Court chambers, the

The Capitol Building.

Brumidi Corridors, and the National Statuary Hall. When you tour the building, you'll see interior embellishments that include richly patterned and colored floor tiles, the vaulted and ornately decorated corridors on the first floor of the Senate wing, and the fluted white marble pillars lining the Hall of Columns, plus hundreds of paintings, sculptures, and other artworks, including the 4,664-square-foot (433-sq.-m) fresco *The Apotheosis of Washington.* In late 2008, visiting the Capitol changed monumentally with the opening of the Capitol Visitor Center. This half billion–dollar complex, located beneath the Capitol itself, has an exhibition hall featuring the Statue of Freedom, amendments to the Constitution, and an 11-foot (3.4m) model of the Capitol Dome. Hands-on exhibits include virtual tours of the building and touchable reproductions of famous Capitol artworks. Food, beverages, large bags, and pointed objects are prohibited on these tours. ⏱ *2 hr. East end of The Mall (entrance on E. Capitol and 1st sts. NW).* ☎ *202/226-8000. www.aoc. gov, www.house.gov, www.visitthe capitol.gov, or www.senate.gov. Free admission. Advance reservations required for tours beyond the Visitor Center. Mon–Sat, 1st tour at 8:50am and last at 3:20pm. Closed Jan 1, Thanksgiving, and Dec 25. Metro: Capitol South or Union Station.*

Legislative Sessions Live

If you wish to visit the House and/or Senate galleries while they are in session, you'll need a pass from your congressional representative, or from your sergeant-at-arms if you live in the District (and suffer "taxation without representation"). The House gallery is open weekdays from 9am to 4:15pm when the House is not in session; the Senate gallery is open during scheduled recesses of 1 week or more, on weekdays from 9am to 4:15pm. Entry to both galleries is through the Capitol Visitor Center on the upper level. (☎ **202/226-8000;** www.visitthecapitol.gov).

② ★★ The Supreme Court. Whether they're debating about constitutionality, voting over dimpled chads, or walking a social tightrope over controversial federal laws, the nation's nine Supreme Court justices, who are appointed for life terms, cast their votes here. The chamber of the highest court in the land has been restored to its mid-19th-century appearance. It's worth visiting, if only to see for yourself how justice prevails—or sometimes doesn't.

The Court convenes on the first Monday in October and stays in session until it has heard all of its cases and handed down its decisions. It hears oral arguments the Monday, Tuesday, and Wedn— of the first 2 w— through April. the arguments they can watch ceedings. **Note.** —— are a legal eagle bent on spending the whole day here, arrive by 8:30am to get in line early; seating is first-come, first-served. ① *2 hr. 1st and E. Capitol sts. NE.* ☎ *202/479-3030. www. supremecourtus.gov. Free admission. Mon–Fri 9am–4:30pm, except federal holidays. Lines can be long; be prepared to wait for up to 1 hr. Metro: Capitol South or Union Station.*

Start at 2 o'13 after crowds p/8

③ Johnny's Half Shell. Head to this lively spot, steps from the Capitol building, for lunch and chances are you'll see political bigwigs hammering out major decisions over crab cakes, chicken, and more. *400 N. Capitol St. NW* ☎ *202/737-0400. www.johnnyshalfshell.net. $–$$. Metro: Union Station.*

④ ★★ International Spy Museum. James Bond, eat your heart out. This place makes your "high-tech" gadgetry seem, well, quaint. Come tour the real deal, the first American museum dedicated to the art of espionage. Learn ——— uble agents, attend ——— tment of expert ——— spy treasures ——— lms, play spy ——— and do other super cool, super sneaky stuff. ① *2 hr. 800 F St. NW.* ☎ *202/EYE-SPYU (393-7798). www.spymuseum.org. Admission $22 adults, $16 seniors, $15 kids 7–11, free for kids 6 and under. Hours change frequently; see website for details. Metro: Gallery Place/ Chinatown.*

⑤ The FBI. The highest level of American law enforcement, the Federal Bureau of Investigation is headquartered on Pennsylvania

Avenue, between 9th and 10th streets, in the J. Edgar Hoover Building. Although it once offered public tours, these have been suspended indefinitely. But that shouldn't stop you from buying an FBI sweatshirt from a street vendor and telling everyone back home you toured it anyway. ⏱ *20 min. 935 Pennsylvania Ave. NW.* ☎ *202/324-3447. www.fbi.gov. Metro: Federal Triangle and Archives*

⑥ The National Archives. One of the best ways to experience the founding of our nation's government is by seeing the documents that started it all. The Constitution, The Declaration of Independence, and The Bill of Rights are here, along with countless other materials such as Abraham Lincoln's telegrams to his generals and audio recordings from the Oval Office. Advance reservations are highly recommended, as lines to get in can stretch as long as an hour during the height of tourist season (Mid-March through Labor Day). Guided tours are offered at 9:45am Monday through Friday, or you can book a Timed Visit Entry, 10am to 90 minutes before closing. ⏱ *1½ hr. Constitution Ave. NW (between 7th & 9th sts.)* ☎ *202/357-5000.*

www.archives.gov. Free admission. Daily 10am–5:30pm. Closed Thanksgiving and Dec. 25. Metro: Archives/ Navy Memorial.

⑦ ★★★ The White House. President John Adams and his wife Abigail were the first tenants back in 1800, and every subsequent U.S. president and his wife have lived here since. President Barack Obama and his wife Michelle planted an organic garden on its lawn and even built a play set for daughters Malia and Sasha on the south grounds. But the White House has seen its share of drama over the years: It endured a fire set by invading British troops in 1812; survived another blaze in 1929 during Herbert Hoover's presidency; lived down President Clinton's Oval Office shenanigans in the late 1990s; and even served as a backdrop for the Aaron Sorkin series, *The West Wing,* taking political drama to an Emmy-winning level. If you wish to tour its legendary rooms—from the elegant reception area of the Blue Room to the Yellow Oval Room, where state guests are entertained before or after official luncheons—you must make an official request and submit it through your member of Congress.

James Bond's Aston Martin at the International Spy Museum.

Aerial view of the White House.

These self-guided tours are scheduled on a first-come, first-served basis and need to be made at least 3 weeks in advance of your visit. To enhance your experience, stop by the White House Visitor Center to view exhibitions on the architecture, furnishings, events, and social history of America's First Address.

🕐 *1 hr.; come early for an unobstructed view through the iron fence and skip any elbowing to get close.* 1600 Pennsylvania Ave. NW. ☎ *202/456-7041 (24-hr. information hotline). www.nps.gov/whho. Free admission. Tour times vary. Visitor center: 1450 Pennsylvania Ave. NW. Open daily 7:30am–4pm. Closed on federal holidays. Metro: Federal Triangle and McPherson Square.*

8️⃣ **BLT Steak.** Legions of downtown officegoers, lawyers, and politicians pack this casual steakhouse, just 1 block from the White House, during weekday lunches. Of course red meat is always on the menu, but so are salads, oysters, and other seafood. Warning: It does get loud. *1625 I St. NW* ☎ *202/689-8999. $$. Metro: Farragut West or Farragut North.*

9️⃣ **Watergate Complex.** Remember when the Watergate Hotel was synonymous only with Nixon, botched burglaries, and Woodward and Bernstein? When you walk by this Washington legend, you can't help but think of another salacious scandal that found its orbit here: The adjacent Watergate condo complex is where Monica Lewinsky hid for 9 months from a stalking press corps after news broke of her affair with President Bill Clinton. She left the residence in October 1998, leaving a note of apology to her neighbors.

🕐 *10 min. Condo complex: 700 New Hampshire Ave. NW. Metro: Foggy Bottom.*

🔟 **Map of the Political Stars.** If you've ever cruised around Beverly Hills, California, you've seen

The infamous Watergate Hotel.

The Pentagon 9/11 Memorial.

the signs selling "Star Maps" that pinpoint the gated entrances to your favorite celebrities' private dwellings. Because Washington has famously been described as "Holly-wood for Ugly People," a map of the political stars seems appropri-ate. Politicos and the journalists who cover them set up house all around the District, but George-town is like the North Star when it comes to finding government types past and present. This tour focuses on this enclave for the rich and powerful—the Beverly Hills of the nation's capital.

⓫ ★★★ **The Pentagon.** The headquarters for the Department of Defense is one of the world's larg-est office buildings, holding approximately 23,000 government workers, both military and civilian. Perhaps only the White House fig-ures as much into the collective consciousness as this structure. It

was scarred on the tragic day of September 11, 2001, when a hijacked airliner ripped into its west side, killing 125 workers and 59 pas-sengers. The building smoldered for days. But, incredibly, the gash in its wall was rebuilt within 6 months and new offices were constructed by the 1-year anniversary of the attack. In dedication to the lives lost in the attack, the Pentagon 9/11 Memorial was constructed and unveiled on September 11, 2008. It consists of 184 benches—one for each victim—with a small reflecting pool beneath each. It's free and open to the public every day. To tour the building, you'll need to reserve a tour at least 3 weeks (and a maximum of 3 months) in advance of your visit. ① *2 hr. including com-mute. Off I-395.* ☎ *703/697-1776. http://pentagontours.osd.mil. To sub-mit your tour request, go to the web site and click "Tours." Free admission. Metro: Pentagon.*

Tudor Place.

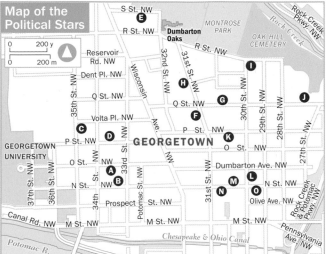

Map of the Political Stars

S St. NW
E
R St. NW
Dumbarton Oaks
MONTROSE PARK
Rock Creek Pkwy. NW
Rock Creek
OAK HILL CEMETERY
R St. NW
Reservoir Rd. NW
Wisconsin
Dent Pl. NW
32nd St. NW
31st St. NW
I
Q St. NW
H
Q St. NW
G
30th St. NW
29th St. NW
28th St. NW
J
Volta Pl. NW
C
D
P St. NW
Wisconsin Ave. NW
P St. NW
GEORGETOWN
F
P St. NW
K
O St. NW
35th St. NW
GEORGETOWN UNIVERSITY
O St. NW
33rd St. NW
Dumbarton Ave. NW
37th St. NW
36th St. NW
N St. NW
A
B
N St. NW
34th St.
Potomac St. NW
Prospect St. NW
31st St. NW
M
L
N St. NW
N
O
Olive Ave. NW
Rock Creek & Potomac Pkwy. NW
Canal Rd. NW
M St. NW
M St. NW
M St. NW
M St. NW
Pennsylvania Ave. NW
Potomac R.
Chesapeake & Ohio Canal

0   200 y
0   200 m

A John Kerry residence A residence of the senator and former presidential candidate (3322 O St. NW). **B John and Jackie Kennedy house.** Their home before moving into the White House (3307 N St. NW). **C Alexander Graham Bell residence.** Home of the inventor of the telephone—not a political figure per se, but one whose contributions were to have a huge impact on the future of the nation (1527 35th St. NW). **D John Edwards residence.** The former senator and his family lived here. Also the former home of CIA head Frank Wisner. Legend has it that many CIA agents lived along Q Street during the Agency's founding years (3327 P St. NW). **E John Warner and Elizabeth Taylor Home**—once upon a time (3240 S St. NW). **F John F. Kennedy residence.** He lived here after first being elected to Congress from Massachusetts's 11th District (1528 31st St. NW). **G Bob Woodward.** Home of the Watergate reporter (3027 Q. St. NW). **H Tudor Place.** Once home to six generations of Martha

Washington's descendants, it's now a museum (1644 31st St. NW). **I Katharine Graham.** Former home of the woman who guided the *Washington Post* for decades (2920 R St. NW). **J Dumbarton House.** Originally belonged to Joseph Nourse, register of the Treasury for six presidents (2715 Q St. NW). **K Henry Kissinger.** Former home of the super-diplomat (3026 P St. NW). **L Miss Lydia English's Georgetown Female Seminary.** Visited by Martin Van Buren, James Buchanan, and Daniel Webster. Later served as a Union Army hospital. (1311 30th St. NW). **M Jackie Kennedy.** She lived here briefly following JFK's assassination (3017 N St. NW). **N Pamela and W. Averell Harriman residence.** Former home of the politician, diplomat, and businessman W. Averell Harriman and his third wife, the socialite and political activist Pamela Churchill Harriman (3038 N St. NW). **O Foxhall House.** Residence of Henry Foxhall, whose foundry provided guns for the War of 1812 (2908 N St. NW). ⏱ **90 min.**

D.C. for Architecture Lovers

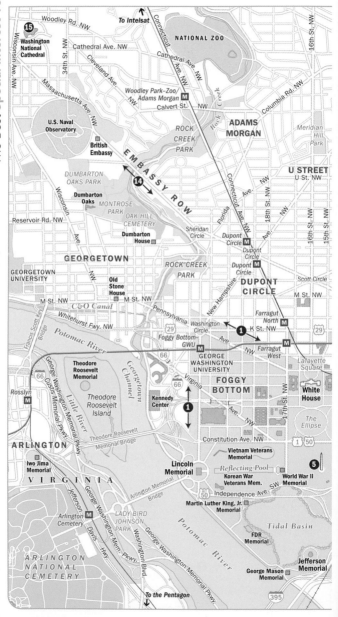

Woodley Rd. NW

To Intelsat

15 Washington National Cathedral

NATIONAL ZOO

Cathedral Ave. NW

Cleveland Ave. NW

Woodley Park-Zoo/ Adams Morgan

Calvert St. NW

ADAMS MORGAN

Meridian Hill Park

U.S. Naval Observatory

ROCK CREEK PARK

British Embassy

E M B A S S Y   R O W

U STREET
U St. NW

DUMBARTON OAKS PARK

14

MONTROSE PARK

Dumbarton Oaks

OAK HILL CEMETERY

Reservoir Rd. NW

Sheridan Circle

Dupont Circle

GEORGETOWN

Dumbarton House

Scott Circle

ROCK CREEK PARK

Dupont Circle

GEORGETOWN UNIVERSITY

Old Stone House

DUPONT CIRCLE

M St. NW

M St. NW

M St. NW

C&O Canal

Whitehurst Fwy. NW

Pennsylvania

Farragut North

K St. NW

1

Washington Circle

Foggy Bottom-GWU

Farragut West

Potomac River

Francis Scott Key Bridge

29

Lafayette Square

GEORGE WASHINGTON UNIVERSITY

66

Theodore Roosevelt Memorial

Georgetown Channel

FOGGY BOTTOM

White House

Rosslyn

66

Kennedy Center

Virginia

The Ellipse

Theodore Roosevelt Island

1

Theodore Roosevelt Memorial Bridge

Constitution Ave. NW

ARLINGTON

Iwo Jima Memorial

VIRGINIA

Little River

Vietnam Veterans Memorial

Reflecting Pool

Lincoln Memorial

World War II Memorial

5

Korean War Veterans Mem.

Arlington Memorial Bridge

Independence Ave. SW

Arlington Cemetery

LADY BIRD JOHNSON PARK

Martin Luther King, Jr. Memorial

Tidal Basin

FDR Memorial

ARLINGTON NATIONAL CEMETERY

Potomac River

George Mason Memorial

Jefferson Memorial

To the Pentagon

395

1 L'Enfant's Grid
2 U.S. Capitol Building
3 The Jefferson Building of the Library of Congress
4 Folger Shakespeare Library
5 Washington Monument
6 National Museum of African American History and Culture
7 Smithsonian Castle
8 National Museum of the American Indian
9 National Gallery of Art
10 National Portrait Gallery
11 National Building Museum
12 Union Station
13 Center Café
14 Embassy Row
15 Washington National Cathedral

Italian journalist Beppe Severgnini wrote Ciao, America: An Italian Discovers the U.S.—which details his experience living in a historic Georgetown row house. He echoes the sentiments I've heard among many expat Europeans in Washington: that despite the stark foreignness of America—the fast-food, techno-obsessed, impatient, kid-worshipping culture of this country—at least, in D.C., there is the architecture. The buildings here evoke the grand structures of Paris and the historically wrought designs of London, with the neoclassical embellishments of both—Roman-style pillars, carved flourishes, and weathered stone lions sitting on guard before public entrances.

START: Metro to Capitol South or Union Station.

① **L'Enfant's Grid.** Designed in 1791 by French engineer Pierre L'Enfant, the District's street plan—a conventional city grid overlaid with grand, diagonal avenues named for U.S. states—mimics the layout of many great European cities. Designed to represent the separation of powers and the balance between state and federal government the grid links the Capitol and the White House via Pennsylvania Avenue. The 2½-mile-long (4km), 400-foot-wide (120m) esplanade known as the National Mall stretches from the Capitol to the Potomac; many iconic museums and monuments sit within its boundaries.

Washington fired L'Enfant, whose grand scheme prevailed but took more than a century to build, with major snafus along the way (such as when the British torched the White House, the

Capitol Building, and the Library of Congress in 1814). But D.C.'s centennial in 1900 brought renewed interest in and commitment to L'Enfant's vision, attracting the likes of Frederick Law Olmstead, Daniel Burnham, and Charles McKim. ⏱ *20 min. To see L'Enfant's original drawings and other historical documents, visit the Library of Congress, p 54.*

② ★★★ **U.S. Capitol Building.** Washington's architecture is about neoclassical harmony and a fierce reverence for the era that birthed the nation's capital, and no building better exemplifies these values than the Capitol itself. Amateur architect George Washington praised the original plans, drafted by Dr. William Thornton, for their "grandeur, simplicity, and convenience." Construction, however, was anything but simple. When Congress first met here in

The rotunda of the U.S. Capitol.

The lavish interior of the Library of Congress.

November 1800, it was still under construction. Begun in 1793, the project would take 34 years and six architects to complete. Even then, it was too small for its occupants, and a second round of construction lasted through 1851. Lincoln insisted that the expansion continue during the Civil War. The neoclassical structure now covers 4 acres (1.6 hectares), and is 288 feet (86m) tall, including the Statue of Freedom. ⏱ *2 hr. See p 17.*

❸ ★ Jefferson Building of the Library of Congress. A much smaller version of the Library of Congress originally sat inside the new Capitol, but the British destroyed it upon sacking the city during the War of 1812. In its place, Thomas Jefferson offered his personal library. In 1886, Congress finally authorized construction of a larger Italian Renaissance–style library, designed by local architects John L. Smithmeyer and Paul J. Pelz. Coming years saw the addition of an equally impressive interior with works by more than 50 American artists, commissioned by architect Edward Pearce Casey. In the Main Reading Room, crane your neck to see the dome 160 feet (48m) above; the cupola is a female figure painted by artist Edwin

Blashfield, representing "Human Understanding." ⏱ *1 hr. 10 First St., SE.* ☎ *202/707-8000. www.loc. gov. Free admission. Obtain same-day free tickets to tour the library inside the west entrance on 1st St. Mon–Fri 8:30am–4:30pm. Closed federal holidays. Metro: Capitol South.*

❹ Folger Shakespeare Library. The marble exterior of this neoclassical building blends harmoniously with the nearby Library of Congress and Supreme Court, but the interior is pure Tudor England, complete with oak paneling and plaster ceilings. The

The Folger Shakespeare Library.

building was designed by Paul Philippe Cret, but the Shakespeare bas-reliefs on the exterior were designed by John Gregory. The library houses the world's largest Shakespeare collection as well as other rare books and manuscripts. ⏱ *30 min. 201 E. Capitol St. SE.* ☎ *202/544-4600. www.folger.edu. Free admission. Mon–Sat 10am–5pm, Sun noon–5pm; free walk-in tours Mon–Sat at 11am, 1pm, and 3pm and on Sun noon and 3pm. Closed federal holidays. Metro: Capitol South or Union Station.*

❺ Washington Monument.
The idea for a national monument to George Washington began as early as 1783, but construction on this Egyptian-style obelisk in the center of the National Mall didn't begin until 1848. Designed by famed architect Robert Mills, work on the monument was stopped in 1854 due to lack of funds. To this day, you can see the difference in color of the marble between the bottom and top. It was the tallest building in the world until the Eiffel Tower's completion in 1889, and it's still the tallest building in D.C. ⏱ *45 min. See p 10.*

The red sandstone exterior of the Smithsonian Castle makes it stand out from its marble neighbors on the Mall.

Fourth of July fireworks exploding over the Mall.

❻ National Museum of African American History and Culture. Occupying the last buildable space on the National Mall, this museum, which opens in 2016, is designed to embody African American heritage in its "tripartite column" construction, following traditional Yoruban art and architecture. Led by architects Philip Freelon and David Adjaye, the bronze top layer of the three-part design allows daylight to enter through patterned openings and skylights. At night, the top glows, offering views of the museum from a variety of vantage points in and around the Mall. As visitors move throughout the museum, a series of openings frame specific views of the city from the inside out. ⏱ *1 hr. 15th and Constitution Aves. NW.* ☎ *202/633-1000. nmaahc.si.edu. Free admission. Daily 10am–5pm. Closed federal holidays. Metro: Smithsonian*

❼ Smithsonian Castle. From museums to monuments, marble is de rigueur for buildings along the National Mall. So no wonder this Gothic castle, placed squarely in the middle of the lot, sticks out. Architect James Renwick, Jr., of St.

Curbing Vertical Sprawl

In 1899, Congress passed the Heights of Building Act, which stipulated that no private structure could rise higher than the Capitol Building or other important government edifice—meaning the skyscrapers of other towns would never stand a chance. (A later act amended this height restriction to 130 ft./39m, and made exceptions for spires, towers, and domes.) This merely challenged contemporary architects to soar to new "heights"; modern design here is concise but nonetheless stunning.

Patrick's Cathedral in New York, designed the original Smithsonian Institution Building in 1855, and constructed it of red sandstone from nearby Seneca Creek, MD. The classic structure is now home base for the Smithsonian Information Center and its gallery. ⏱ *30 min. 1000 Jefferson Dr. SW.* ☎ *202/633-1000. www.si.edu. Free admission. Daily, 8:30am–5:30pm. Closed Dec. 25. Metro: Smithsonian.*

❽ ★★ National Museum of the American Indian. A team of Native American architects and consultants designed this pueblo-looking museum, constructed of Kasota stone, on the National Mall. With its curved facade and angled placement, the building aligns with Native American beliefs in the cardinal points. The grounds include cascading water, as well as wetlands of wild rice, marsh marigolds, corn, native tree species, and indigenous plants to honor local Native people. ⏱ *1½ hrs. 4th St. & Independence Ave. SW.* ☎ *202/633-1000. Free admission. Daily 10am–5:30pm. Closed Dec. 25. www.nmai.si.edu. Metro: L'Enfant Plaza.*

❾ The National Gallery of Art. The museum's triangular-shaped East Building—with its acute-angled stone corners, designed in 1978 by I. M. Pei—may look worlds apart from the neoclassical West Building across the plaza, but its marble was cut from the same quarry in Tennessee. The

The National Gallery of Art's East Building.

West Building, which resembles the nearby Museum of Natural History, was designed by John Russell Pope in 1941. ○ *1 hr. See p 72.*

⑩ ★★★ **National Portrait Gallery.** Designed by a number of prominent architects, including Robert Mills (designer of the Washington Monument), this museum was the third public building constructed in the city, after the Capitol and the White House. During the Civil War, it served as the site of Lincoln's second inaugural ball as well as a hospital for soldiers. Although it's a notable example of Greek Revival architecture, it was almost demolished in the 1950s before the Smithsonian Institution took over its control. It closed in 2001 for a 5-year renovation project that added more exhibition space, an auditorium, and an enclosed courtyard featuring a dramatic glass-and-steel roof. ○ *1 hr. 8th and F sts. NW (in the U.S. Patent Office Building).* ☎ *202/638-8300. www.npg.si.edu. Free admission. Daily 11:30am–7pm. Closed Dec. 25. Metro: Gallery Place/Chinatown.*

⑪ **National Building Museum.** With regular exhibitions devoted to art and architecture, this palatial brick museum took roughly 5 years

The Kogod Courtyard at the National Portrait Gallery.

to build, and was modeled after Italy's monumental Palazzo Farnese that Michelangelo commissioned in 1589. The massive Great Hall of the building holds colossal Corinthian columns—among the tallest in the world. A fountain bisects the hall, stretching 28 feet (8.5m) across. Strategically placed windows, vents, and archways are part of a unique ventilation system that whisks a continuous flow of fresh air through the building. ○ *1 hr. 401 F St. NW.* ☎ *202/272-2448. $10 adults; $7 youth, students, and seniors. $3 general, ages 3 and up, entrance to the Building Zone* only (appropriate for ages 2–6). Mon–Sat, 10am–5pm, Sun 11am–5pm. www.nbm.org. Metro: Judiciary Square.*

⑫ **Union Station.** When master architect Daniel Burnham designed this Beaux Arts–style building, he was determined to make it a grand gateway for a magnificent city, complete with 96-foot (29m) ceilings inlaid with 70 pounds (32 kilograms) of 22-karat gold leaf. Upon its completion in 1908, Union Station was the largest train station in the world; if laid on its side, the Washington Monument would fit into its concourse. Its original area, along with the terminal zone, totaled 200 acres (80 hectares) and included 75 miles (121km) of track. It was also enormously expensive, costing roughly $125 million to build. ○ *45 min. 50 Massachusetts Ave. NE.* ☎ *202/289-1908. www.unionstationdc.com. Free admission. Daily 24 hr. Metro: Union Station.*

⑬ **Center Café.** Linger over the view of Union Station's opulent atrium while enjoying a few quick bites of American fare. *Union Station, 50 Massachusetts Ave. NE;* ☎ *202/682-0143; http://arkrestaurants.com/center_cafe.html. $. Metro: Union Station.*

The British Embassy.

⑭ ★★ Embassy Row. This stretch of Massachusetts Avenue, from Dupont Circle to the National Cathedral, is where the majority of foreign embassies and ambassadors reside. Sir Edwin Lutyens—an architect of the late 19th and early 20th centuries, renowned for his English country houses and remodeled castles—designed The British Embassy in 1928. This prominent Embassy Row structure is notable for its tall chimneys and high roofs, suggestive of the Queen Anne period. From this traditional design to the contemporary glass wall that juts over Rock Creek Park at the Finnish embassy, there's no shortage of architectural inspiration along this avenue. ⏱ *2 hr. Begin: Massachusetts Ave. NW at Dupont Circle and head North. Metro: Dupont Circle.*

⑮ ★★★ National Cathedral. More than 200 stained glass windows adorn this classic Gothic-style cathedral, the second largest in the United States and sixth largest in the world; one of them has a rock from the moon embedded in its center. The building, made largely of gray Indiana limestone and finally completed in 1990 after more than 80 years of work and 2 centuries of planning, contains a number of magnificent wood carvings, metal work, and other artworks. Frederick Bodley, an Anglican Church architect, originally oversaw the project (with additional supervision by architect Henry Vaughan), but Philip Hubert Frohman took over after World War I. The top of the cathedral tower is the highest point in the city. ⏱ *1 hr.* *See p 21.*

Washington for Kids

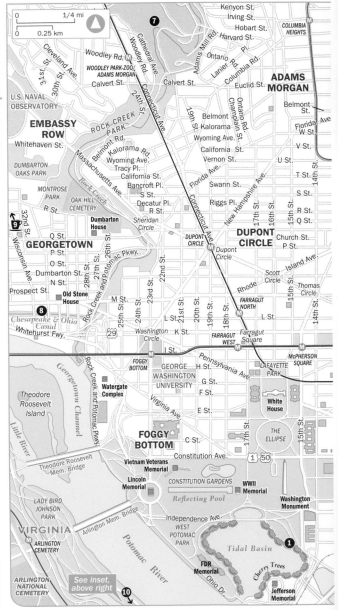

ROCK CREEK PARK

White House

Union Station

Area of main map

NATIONAL MALL

Lincoln Memorial

U.S. Capitol

ARLINGTON NATIONAL CEMETERY

The Pentagon

VIRGINIA

Potomac River

Reagan Nat'l Airport

10

D.C. Area

Kenyon St.
Irving St.
Columbia Rd.
Harvard St.
Girard St.
Fairmont St.
Euclid St.

HOWARD UNIVERSITY

13th St.
12th St.
11th St.
10th St.
9th St.
8th St.

Barry Pl.

U STREET CORRIDOR

U STREET-CARDOZO

SHAW-HOWARD UNIVERSITY

Rhode Island Ave.

Logan Circle

7th St.
6th St.
5th St.
4th St.
3rd St.

29
1

North Capitol St.

Florida Ave.

BRENTWOOD PARK

13th St.
12th St.
11th St.
10th St.
9th St.
8th St.

N St.

M St.

New York Ave.

50

New Jersey Ave.

DOWNTOWN

Mt. Vernon Square

MT. VERNON SQ./ CONVENTION CTR.

1

New York Ave.

1

CHINATOWN

Massachusetts

395

K St.

I St.

H St.

G St.

1st St.

UNION STATION

METRO CENTER

GALLERY PLACE-CHINATOWN

5

2

3rd St.
2nd St.

Ave.

F St.

E St.

Union Station

PENN QUARTER

6

JUDICIARY SQUARE

D St.

Louisiana Ave.

Delaware Ave.

FEDERAL TRIANGLE

Pennsylvania Ave.

C St.

Stanton Square

Maryland

3

ARCHIVES-NAVY MEMORIAL

Constitution Ave.

A St.

CAPITOL HILL

East Capitol St.

A St.

NATIONAL MALL

SMITHSONIAN

Madison Dr.

U.S. Capitol

4

Jefferson Dr.

Independence Ave.

L'ENFANT PLAZA

FEDERAL CENTER SW

Washington Ave.

New Jersey Ave.

CAPITOL SOUTH

Seward Square

North Carolina Ave.

Pennsylvania Ave.

EASTERN MARKET

Washington Channel

395

South Capitol St.

1 Tidal Basin

2 National Building Museum

3 National Museum of Natural History

4 National Air and Space Museum

5 International Spy Museum

6 District Chophouse

7 National Zoological Park

8 C&O Canal Towpath

9 2 Amys

10 Gravelly Point

Here's a bold statement: There is no better place to take the kids on vacation than Washington, D.C. The District is overflowing with the stuff of a memorable field trip—pandas, dinosaur bones, spy gadgets, rocket ships, insect gardens, historic monuments—and much of it is free. There's even a park, adjacent to Ronald Reagan National Airport, that's so close to the runways, you feel as though planes are landing on top of you. Ask any kid—nothing is cooler than this. Allow at least 2 days to complete this tour, or pick and choose the stops you wish to visit, depending on your kids' attention span and level of interest. START: **Metro to Smithsonian.**

❶ ★★★ Paddling the Tidal Basin.
The Jefferson Memorial overlooks the serene waters of the Tidal Basin, dotted with paddleboats on sunny days. Rent a boat and marry a history lesson with great exercise—and see the monuments and cherry blossoms from a beautiful, unique vantage point. ⏱ *1 hr. 1501 Maine Ave. SW (15th St.).* ☎ *202/479-2426. www.tidal basinpaddleboats.com. 2-passenger boat $15 per hr.; 4-passenger boat $24 per hr. Mar 15 to mid-Oct daily 10am–6pm. Metro: Smithsonian.*

Paddle boats on the Tidal Basin.

❷ ★★ The National Building Museum.
If the weather is blistering or freezing, and the kids need to blow off some steam, then head to this museum. The colossal Great Hall, which has hosted 15 presidential inaugural balls, is the perfect place to let them run indoors. Bring your own food and have a picnic inside, or head to the museum's Building Zone, ideal for visitors ages 2 to 6. Children can build towers and walls, drive bulldozers, or work on any number of arts and crafts projects. ⏱ *1 hr. 401 F St. NW* ☎ *202/272-2448. www.nbm. org. Adults $10; youth, students, and seniors, $7; Building Zone entrance only, $3. Mon–Sat 10am–5pm, Sun 11am–5pm. Metro: Judiciary Square or Gallery Place/Chinatown.*

❸ ★★ National Museum of Natural History.
Opened in 1910, this enormous repository for animal and plant specimens, many long extinct, includes a T. Rex skull, fossils, the Hope Diamond, and the remains of a Giant Squid—guaranteed to wow even the most Nintendo-obsessed kids. While the National Fossil Hall is closed for renovations until 2019, kids can still see fossilized dinosaurs and learn more about the giants that once roamed the Earth on the second floor of the museum. Everyone loves the huge African bush elephant that greets you at the Mall-facing entrance, the expansive Sant Ocean Hall with its 674 marine specimens, and the first floor Discovery Room filled with creative, hands-on exhibits "for children of all ages." The outdoor Butterfly Habitat Garden, on the 9th Street side of the building, is another

crowd-pleaser: The 11,000 square feet (1,022 sq. m) area of winding trails and lush vegetation supports an estimated 22 species of butterflies. The garden cultivates interaction between these winged creatures and the plants and flowers that attract them, educating and delighting visitors. ⏱ *1 hr. 10th St. and Constitution Ave. NW ☎ 202/633-1000. www.mnh.si.edu. Free admission. Daily 10am–5:30pm (Until 7:30pm on select dates). Closed Dec 25. Metro: Smithsonian or Federal Triangle.*

National Museum of Natural History.

④ ★★★ National Air and Space Museum. Containing the largest historic collection of air- and spacecraft in the world, this is the place to explore rocket ships that have shot to the stars, see real Russian and American spacesuits, view the 1903 Wright Brothers' Flyer and World War II bombers, even inspect the earliest passenger planes (kids can walk through the fuselage of one). The number of crafts suspended from the sky-high ceiling inspires lots of upturned heads and dropped jaws. The Lockheed Martin IMAX Theater, with its awesome 3-D effects, will transport your little

A ride on the National Mall carousel makes a great break in between museum-hopping.

ones to Mars or the moon. ⏱ *2 hr. Independence Ave. at 6th St. SW ☎ 202/633-2214. www.nasm.si.edu. Free admission. Daily 10am–5:30pm (until 7:30pm in summer), except Dec 25. Metro: Smithsonian or L'Enfant Plaza (Smithsonian Museums/ Maryland Ave. exit).*

⑤ ★★ International Spy Museum. Older kids who think the zoo is for babies will love this place, the sole public museum dedicated to espionage in the world. They'll learn about Soviet double agents, view the spy treasures from Hollywood films, play spy games, watch informative films, and take part in other super-sneaky stuff in a range of interactive exhibits. An executive director who spent 36 years with the CIA and an advisory board including two former CIA directors, two former CIA disguise chiefs, and a retired KGB general ensure that the stuff you see here is 100% authoritative. ⏱ *1 hr. Metro: Gallery Place/Chinatown. See p 94.*

⑥ District Chophouse and Brewery. Just 2 blocks from the Spy Museum, this eatery offers a little of everything: salads, soups, sandwiches, crab cakes, and pizzas, plus handcrafted ales brewed on site. *509 7th St. NW ☎ 202/347-3434. www.districtchophouse.com. $.*

46

The Best Special-Interest Tours

❼ ★★★ National Zoological Park. Established in 1889, the National Zoo is home to some 500 species, many of them rare and/or endangered. It also occupies 163 acres (65 hectares) of beautifully landscaped and wooded land, wonderful for strolling and enjoying the sunshine. Start your tour with the famous pandas. ⏱ *2 hr. See p 15.*

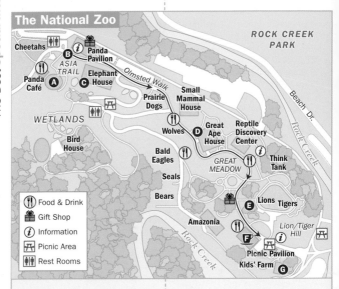

The National Zoo

ROCK CREEK PARK

Cheetahs

Panda Pavilion

ASIA TRAIL

Panda Café **A**

Elephant House **C**

Olmsted Walk

WETLANDS

Prairie Dogs

Small Mammal House

Bird House

Wolves **D**

Great Ape House

Reptile Discovery Center

Bald Eagles

GREAT MEADOW

Think Tank

Seals

Bears

Lions **E** Tigers

Amazonia

F

Lion/Tiger Hill

Picnic Pavilion

Kids' Farm **G**

Beach Dr.

Rock Creek

🍴 Food & Drink
🎁 Gift Shop
ⓘ Information
🏕 Picnic Area
🚻 Rest Rooms

Arguably the stars of the zoo, the giant pandas Mei Xiang and Tian Tian take center stage at the zoo's **❼A David M. Rubenstein Giant Panda Habitat.** Kids can't get enough of this animated pair, along with Bao Bao and her new addition, Bei Bei. Follow **❼B Olmsted Walk** and you'll spot several natural habitats holding cheetahs, zebras, and bears. An improved home for the **❼C Asian elephants,** complete with a new elephant barn, two outdoor yards and an Elephant Exercise Trek, is now in place. Off the main drag, you'll find natural wetlands and creatures ranging from bald eagles and wolves to sea lions along the American Trail. Farther south, at the **❼D Great Ape House,** you can peer through glass walls at six gorillas as they engage in startlingly humanlike behaviors: grooming, wrestling, and even hugging one another. In the circular habitat of the **❼E Great Cats,** south of the Great Ape House, lions and tigers sun themselves, their tails batting lazily as they gaze out at you. Stop for a bite at the cafeteria-style **❼F Mane Grill,** which offers burgers, fries, salads, chicken sandwiches, and fast-food fare. Dine in, or enjoy the nearby Picnic Pavilion. At the **❼G Kids' Farm,** children 3 to 8 can meet and greet ducks, chickens, goats, cows, and miniature donkeys. Toddlers love the nearby "pizza" playground.

Get an unbeatable view of planes coming in for a landing at Reagan Airport from Gravelly Point.

⑧ C&O Canal Towpath. Have rambunctious little ones? Rent a bike at any nearby outfitter (see p 119 for specifics) and hit the C&O Canal Towpath. The tree-lined, gravelly trail follows a 19th-century canal that begins in Georgetown and heads west, ending 184 miles (296km) later in Cumberland, Maryland. It's a favorite of hikers, joggers, and bicyclists alike; if you're looking to escape the bustle of the city or blow off steam after a day spent touring museums, you'll love it too. Two boat rental outfits near the start of the path rent kayaks and canoes. ◷ *2 hr. See p 119.*

⑨ ★ 2 Amys. The kids **can dig into** authentic Neapolitan pizza while the grown-ups savor lovely Italian red wine by the glass. *3715 Macomb St. NW.* ☎ *202/885-5700. www.2amysdc.com. $$–$$$. No Metro access (a taxi is advised).*

⑩ Gravelly Point. If your kids are thrill-seekers, drive to this park that borders Reagan National Airport, minutes outside the District. (You'll need a car because no return

taxis are available.) On any given day, you'll find teenagers, toddlers, and grandparents parked or picnicking on the grass, just feet from the airport runways. Gaze upward as jet after jet descends and flies directly overhead, so close you can read the markings on its underbelly—and then lands safely a short distance away. Not for the faint of heart! ◷ *2 hr. including commute. Off the northbound George Washington Pkwy.* ☎ *703/289-2500.*

Tian Tian the panda is one of the National Zoo's most popular residents.

Historic Washington

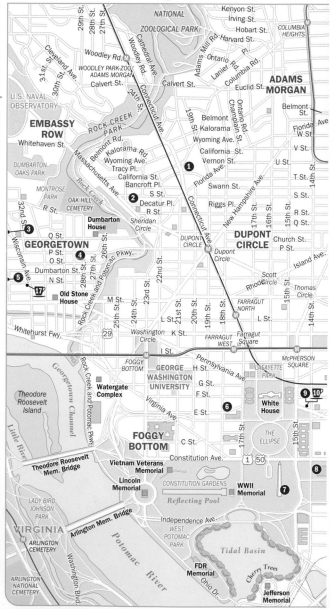

NATIONAL ZOOLOGICAL PARK

Kenyon St.
Irving St.
Hobart St.
Harvard St.

COLUMBIA HEIGHTS

Woodley Rd.

WOODLEY PARK-ZOO
ADAMS MORGAN
Calvert St.

Calvert St.

ADAMS MORGAN

U.S. NAVAL OBSERVATORY

Cleveland Ave.
31st St.
30th St.

EMBASSY ROW

Whitehaven St.

ROCK CREEK PARK

Belmont Rd.
Kalorama Rd.
Wyoming Ave.
Tracy Pl.
Kalorama St.
California St.
Bancroft Pl.
S St.
Decatur Pl.
R St.

Belmont St.
Kalorama
Wyoming Ave.
California St.
Vernon St.

Florida Ave.
Swann St.

Belmont St.
Florida Ave.
W St.
V St.
U St.
T St.
S St.

DUMBARTON OAKS PARK

MONTROSE PARK

OAK HILL CEMETERY

R St.

Dumbarton House

Sheridan Circle

Riggs Pl.

New Hampshire Ave.

17th St.
16th St.
15th St.

R St.
Q St.

❶

❷

❸

32nd St.

Q St.

GEORGETOWN

P St.
O St.

Wisconsin Ave.

Dumbarton St.
N St.

❹

28th St.
27th St.
26th St.

DUPONT CIRCLE

Dupont Circle

Church St.
P St.

DUPONT CIRCLE

Island Ave.

❺

17

Old Stone House

M St.

25th St.
24th St.
23rd St.
22nd St.
21st St.
20th St.
19th St.
18th St.

L St.

Scott Circle
Rhode Island Ave.

Thomas Circle

FARRAGUT NORTH

14th St.

Whitehurst Fwy.

29

Rock Creek and Potomac Pkwy.

Washington Circle

K St.
L St.

FARRAGUT WEST

Farragut Square

I St.

Pennsylvania Ave.

LAFAYETTE PARK

McPHERSON SQUARE

Georgetown Channel

FOGGY BOTTOM

GEORGE WASHINGTON UNIVERSITY

H St.
G St.
F St.
E St.

Watergate Complex

Virginia Ave.

❻

White House

THE ELLIPSE

❾ **10**

17th St.
15th St.

❽

Theodore Roosevelt Island

Little River

Theodore Roosevelt Mem. Bridge

FOGGY BOTTOM

C St.

Constitution Ave.

1 50

❼

Rock Creek and Potomac Pkwy.

Vietnam Veterans Memorial

Lincoln Memorial

CONSTITUTION GARDENS

Reflecting Pool

WWII Memorial

LADY BIRD JOHNSON PARK

VIRGINIA

ARLINGTON CEMETERY

ARLINGTON NATIONAL CEMETERY

Arlington Mem. Bridge

Washington Blvd.

Independence Ave.

WEST POTOMAC PARK

Potomac River

FDR Memorial

Ohio Dr.

Tidal Basin

Cherry Trees

Jefferson Memorial

D.C. Area

Area of
main map

ROCK
CREEK
PARK

White
House

Union
Station

NATIONAL MALL

Lincoln
Memorial

U.S. Capitol

ARLINGTON
NATIONAL
CEMETERY

VIRGINIA

The Pentagon

15 ANACOSTIA

Reagan Nat'l
Airport

1. Hilton Washington
2. Woodrow Wilson House
3. 3321 Dent Place
4. 2808 P St
5. 3307 N St
6. Octagon Museum
7. Washington Monument
8. Star-Spangled Banner
9. Willard InterContinental
10. The Occidental
11. Ford's Theatre
   National Historic Site
12. National Portrait Gallery
13. Sewall-Belmont House
14. Library of Congress
15. Frederick Douglass
   National Historic Site
16. Lincoln's Cottage
17. Martin's Tavern

U STREET
CORRIDOR
U STREET-
CARDOZO

Kenyon St.
Irving St.
Columbia Rd.
Harvard St.
Girard St.
Fairmont St.
Euclid St.

HOWARD
UNIVERSITY

13th St.
12th St.
11th St.
10th St.
9th St.
8th St.

Barry Pl.

French St.

SHAW-
HOWARD UNIVERSITY

Rhode Island Ave.

7th St.
6th St.
5th St.
4th St.
3rd St.

Florida Ave.

Logan
Circle

29

1

DOWNTOWN

13th St.
12th St.
11th St.
10th St.
9th St.
8th St.

N St.

M St.

New York Ave.

North Capitol St.

Mt. Vernon
Square

MT. VERNON SQ./
CONVENTION CTR.

1

50

Massachusetts

New Jersey Ave.

395

K St.

I St.

H St.

G St.

UNION
STATION

New
York Ave.

1

50

CHINATOWN

GALLERY PLACE-
CHINATOWN

3rd St.
2nd St.
1st St.

F St.

E St.

METRO
CENTER

12

11

PENN
QUARTER

JUDICIARY
SQUARE

D St.

Pennsylvania Ave.

C St.

Louisiana Ave.

Stanton
Square

FEDERAL
TRIANGLE

ARCHIVES-NAVY
MEMORIAL

Constitution Ave.

13

Maryland Ave.

A St.

NATIONAL
MALL

Madison Dr.

U.S. Capitol

CAPITOL
HILL

East Capitol St.

SMITHSONIAN

Jefferson Dr.

14

A St.

Independence Ave.

Washington Ave.

New Jersey Ave.

North Carolina Ave.

L'ENFANT
PLAZA

FEDERAL
CENTER SW

CAPITOL
SOUTH

Seward
Square

Pennsylvania Ave.

EASTERN
MARKET

Washington
Channel

0   1/4 mi

0   0.25 km

395

South Capitol St.

See inset,
above right

15

16

17

In the 21st century, America's capital city bears little resemblance to the swampy Potomac River Valley territory that President George Washington staked out as the new site for Congress in 1790. Yet trying to separate Washington from its past is like trying to take the red from blood. Because of its significance in U.S. history, Washington exists on two planes in the collective consciousness: first, as a real city with magnificent structures and whimsical cherry trees juxtaposed against a backdrop of still-recovering pockets of poverty; and second, as a virtual city of suspenseful Hollywood lore, with its Deep Throat–esque covert operations, war games, and congressional plots. The true Washington lies somewhere between fact and fiction, past and present, and that is why it never loses its intrigue or its allure. You can modify this tour to fit your schedule and level of interest, but allow several days if you wish to visit every stop. **START: Metro to Smithsonian.**

❶ ★★ Hilton Washington. In 1981, John Hinckley, Jr., an obsessed fan of actress Jodie Foster, ambushed Ronald Reagan here, just 69 days into the president's first term, in a misguided attempt to impress the star. Hinckley fired six shots, one of which struck Reagan's armpit. (Reagan's press secretary James Brady was also seriously injured; paralyzed from the waist down.) The Secret Service whisked Reagan away to a waiting hospital, where he underwent emergency surgery, making the now-legendary joke to his doctors: "I hope you're all Republicans." Despite being 70, the president recovered quickly—and went on to tackle other concerns, like the Cold War. ⏱ *30 min. 1919 Connecticut Ave. NW.* ☎ *202/483-3000. www.hilton.com. Metro: Dupont Circle.*

❷ Woodrow Wilson House. This final residence of Nobel Peace Prize winner and 28th President Woodrow Wilson has been preserved to celebrate the great man's "Washington years," from 1913 to 1924. It is where he returned to civilian life after his 8-year term guiding Americans through World War I, giving women the right to vote, and launching the League of Nations (now known as the United Nations). He lived the last 3 years of his life at this grand brick house. Inside, tour his drawing room, kitchen, bedrooms, and garden. *See p 85,* ❸.

❸ 3321 Dent Place. If you are a JFK buff, you'll want to explore both the east and west villages of Georgetown—Wisconsin Avenue divides the historic neighborhood into two enclaves—to check out where the 35th president once lived, in some cases with his glamorous wife, Jackie, and their two children, Caroline and John, Jr. Between January and June 1954, 3321 Dent Place was the first home of Senator and Mrs. Kennedy after their marriage in September 1953. ⏱ *10 min.*

❹ 2808 P St. After a stint in Virginia, the Kennedys moved back to Georgetown, to this tony address, where they lived from January to May 1957. ⏱ *10 min.*

❺ 3307 N St. JFK purchased this home and presented it to Mrs. Kennedy after the birth of their daughter, Caroline. From here, they moved to the White House on January 20, 1961. ⏱ *10 min.*

The Octagon Museum.

6 Octagon Museum. The Octagon is one of the oddest-looking buildings in downtown D.C., and its history is just as intriguing. Built in 1799 for the Tayloe family, the building served as a temporary home to James and Dolley Madison after the British burned the White House in 1814. Ironically, the Treaty of Ghent, ending war with Great Britain, was signed on its second floor. The Octagon was also a girls' school and a tenement, and is presently home to the Architect's Foundation. ⏱ *1 hr. 1799 New York Ave. NW.* ☎ *202/626-7439. www. theoctagon.org. Metro: Farragut West.*

7 ★★ Washington Monument. In 1838, architect Robert Mills designed the largest—and perhaps most famous—masonry structure in the world, the 550-foot (165m) Washington Monument honoring George Washington. While it now resembles a solitary and unadorned Egyptian obelisk, Mills originally intended the marble shaft to rise from a circular building containing a huge statue of the first American president. After much bickering over the design, years of construction, and halted progress during the Civil War (which led to its two-tone marble effect, still

visible today), the monument was finally completed and opened to the public on October 9, 1888. Take the high-speed elevator to the top for a birds-eye view of the National Mall and D.C. from the monument's museum. ⏱ *1 hr. 15th St. SW.* ☎ *202/426-6841, or 800/967-2283 (for reservations). Free timed tickets are available at the 15th Street kiosk on a first-come, first-served basis. Advance tickets are available through the National Park Service. Tickets required for everyone 2 and up. Daily 9am–5pm. Closed July 4 and Dec 25. Metro: Smithsonian.*

8 ★★★ The Star-Spangled Banner. O, say can you see the garrison flag that has come to represent our country and its democratic ideals? You'll find it and its companion exhibit, "The Flag That Inspired the National Anthem," at the National Museum of American History. Backstory: In 1814, Francis Scott Key peered through the clearing smoke after a 25-hour British bombardment of Baltimore's Fort McHenry and saw this very flag flapping proudly in the wind. He immediately wrote a poem that was set to music and sung at the country's patriotic events ever after. In 1907, the worn and tattered but powerfully symbolic flag was

Walk Through History

Cultural Tourism DC offers a series of self-guided walking tours all around the District. Routes include the U Street Heritage Trail, where visitors follow numbered signs with information about this historic neighborhood; the Downtown Heritage Trail, which guides tourists though high and low points in D.C. history, from the Civil War through the civil rights era; and the Adams-Morgan Heritage Trail, a walk through this vibrant community of artists, immigrants, and start-up entrepreneurs. For details, check out www.cultural tourismdc.org.

donated to the museum; in 1931, the song became our national anthem. After undergoing several years of preservation, the flag is now resting in its new high-tech atrium in the museum, designed to keep it carefully protected but still allow throngs of visitors to see this American monument. ⏱ *30 min. 14th St. and Constitution Ave. NW.* ☎ *202/633-1000. http://american history.si.edu. Free admission. Daily 10am–5:30pm (until 7:30pm in summer). Metro: Smithsonian and Federal Triangle.*

The Star-Spangled Banner exhibit at the National Museum of American History.

❾ Willard InterContinental.
Beaux-Arts architecture meets history at the formal, elegant Willard Inter-Continental, which has welcomed almost every president since its 1818 opening, from Franklin Pierce on. It is the place where the Rev. Martin Luther King, Jr., wrote his legendary "I Have a Dream" speech. President Ulysses S. Grant held frequent meetings in the hotel lobby, and a host of celebrity visitors from Walt Whitman to P.T. Barnum have also overnighted here. Steven Spielberg even shot the final scene of The Minority Report with contemporary Hollywood heavyweight Tom Cruise here. It's worth ducking inside to admire the awe-inspiring lobby. ⏱ *15 min. See p 168.*

❿ ★★ Occidental. Adjacent to the Willard InterContinental, this restaurant has been around since 1906. Join the lunchtime rush and admire the autographed photos of guests such as Franklin D. Roosevelt, Amelia Earhart, Robert Frost, and Calvin Coolidge that adorn the walls. *1475 Pennsylvania Ave. NW (at 14th St.)* ☎ *202/783-1475. www. occidentaldc.com. $$$$. Metro: Metro Center.*

⓫ ★★ Ford's Theatre & Lincoln Museum.

Another shot heard round the world was fired here on April 14, 1865, when President Abraham Lincoln was killed as he watched a performance of *Our American Cousin*. The theatre was immediately closed, and remained so for another 103 years. In 1968, it reopened as a living, working tribute to the late leader, serving as a functioning playhouse as well as a repository for historic materials such as assassin John Wilkes Booth's Derringer pistol, the gun that killed the president. In 2006, the theatre closed once again for renovations and reopened in early 2009, with an expanded museum on the president, plus a new lobby, box office, and seating. ○ *1½ hr., or more if you plan to see a show. 511 10th St. NW.* ☎ *202/347-4833. www.fords.org. Standard Museum Admission: $4.25. Performance ticket price varies. Hours vary; check web site for details. Closed Dec. 25. Metro: Metro Center.*

Ford's Theatre, where Abraham Lincoln was assassinated.

⓬ ★★★ National Portrait Gallery.

While the building itself has a rich history—it served as the National Patent Office for 92 years—the Gallery's contents might be considered even more important. Some of the most treasured paintings, sculptures, and artifacts from American history are housed in this ode to the presidents, first ladies, and stars. See the original Gilbert Stuart portrait of George Washington, saved by Dolley Madison in the War of 1812, along with modern depictions of Richard Nixon, John F. Kennedy, and Barack Obama. *8th and F sts., NW.* ☎ *202/633-8300. www.npg.si.edu. Free admission. Daily 11:30am–7pm. Closed Dec. 25. Metro: Gallery Place/Chinatown.*

⓭ Sewall-Belmont House.

Including the works and words of "radicals" such as Susan B.

The Willard Hotel.

Anthony and Gloria Steinem, this museum traces the evolution of a revolution—the women's movement, in all of its fits, starts, and back-and-forward progress. Check out authentic picketing banners, 5,000 prints and photographs, original cartoons, more than 50 scrapbooks from early suffragists, paintings, sculptures, publications, and more. ⏱ *1 hr. (by docent tour only). See p 97.*

⑭ ★ Library of Congress.

Original presidential documents, plus photographs, multimedia, and more can be found at the Library of Congress, which houses the most comprehensive collection of archival material documenting the United States of America's birth and growth as a nation. It occupies three adjacent buildings on Capitol Hill: the Thomas Jefferson Building (1897), the John C. Adams Building (1938), and the James Madison Building (1981). ⏱ *1 hr. 101 Independence Ave. SE. www.loc.gov. Mon–Fri 8:30am–5pm, except federal holidays. Docent-led, scheduled public tours depart from the Great Hall of the Thomas Jefferson Building at 10:30, 11:30am, 12:30, 1:30, 2:30,*

The Sewall-Belmont mansion.

Frederick Douglass National Historic Site.

and 3:30pm. No 3:30pm tour on Saturdays. Arrive 30 min. before start of tour. Metro: Capitol South or Union Station.

⑮ Frederick Douglass National Historic Site.

Born a slave, Frederick Douglass escaped his circumstances to become, as President Lincoln once said, "the most meritorious man" of the 19th century. An outspoken abolitionist, a feminist, a human-rights pioneer, an ambassador, a minister, a family man, and the father of the civil rights movement, Douglass settled here in southeast D.C. at a home he called Cedar Hill, where his personal belongings are now on display. National Park Service rangers lead tours of the house, sharing the stories and legacy of this important American icon. *1411 W St. SE. ☎ 202/426-5961. Free admission. Daily Apr 1–Oct 31 9am–5pm. Nov 1–Mar 31 9am–4:30pm. Closed Jan 1, Thanksgiving, and Dec 25. Metro: Anacostia, then bus no. 2 to "Mt. Rainier", which stops in front of the house.*

Mount Vernon

Easily accessible from the District, **George Washington's Mount Vernon Estate and Gardens,** 3200 Mount Vernon Memorial Hwy. (☎ **703/780-2000;** www.mountvernon.org), is 15 miles (26 km) south of the capital. Educational and appealing to kids and adults alike, this impressive historic homestead is where the first president and his wife, Martha, lived from their wedding in 1759 until Washington's death 40 years later. Tour the main house and see Washington's library, the dining room and parlors, and the bedrooms. The plantation's outbuildings include the kitchen, smokehouse, storeroom, overseer's house, and the cramped slaves' quarters, a somber testament to a dark period in U.S. history. An on-site museum and visitors center has more than 700 artifacts from the Washington family including furnishings, china, silver, clothing, jewelry—even Revolutionary War artifacts and rare books. Activities, from musical events to garden parties, take place year-round. To reach Mount Vernon, take the Metro Rail Yellow Line (☎ **202/637-7000;** www.wmata.com) to Huntington Station, VA. Exit at the lower level to catch a Fairfax Connector (☎ **703/339-7200**) bus no. 101 (Fort Hunt Line) for the 20-min. trip to Mount Vernon. Admission is $17 adults, $16 seniors, $9 kids 6 to 11, and free for kids under 5. The site is open to visitors April to August 8am to 5pm daily, March and September to October 9am to 5pm daily, and November to February 9am to 4pm daily.

George Washington's Mount Vernon Estate.

President Lincoln and his family spent the sweltering D.C. summers at this cottage.

⑯ ★★ President Lincoln's Cottage. When the sweltering heat of D.C. got to be too much for President Lincoln and his family, they retreated to this cottage, originally known as the Soldier's Home. Each June through November during 1862 to 1864, the Lincolns would take in the cool breezes at this house, on the third highest area in Washington, 3 miles (5km) north of what was then downtown. After a restoration by the National Trust for Historic Preservation, this presidential landmark debuted to the public in 2008 and began offering 1-hour guided tours. The cottage is a straight shot up the Green Line on the Metro, and is well worth the detour if you can spare the time. ⏱ *2 hr., including commute. Rock Creek Church Rd. NW and Upshur St. NW. ☎ 202-829-0436. Adults $15, children 6–12 $5. Advance tickets recommended. Metro: Georgia Avenue/Petworth then taxi (to the Armed Forces Retirement Home campus, Eagle Gate entrance).*

⑰ Martin's Tavern. Tuck into a booth at this Georgetown stalwart and you'll be transported to a time when Harry Truman, Lyndon Johnson, and even Richard Nixon regularly held court in the tiny pub. Opened in 1933 and still owned by the Martin family, it's a regular with the locals. Don't miss the "proposal" booth, where JFK is rumored to have proposed to Jackie. *1264 Wisconsin Ave., NW; ☎ 202/333-7370. www.martins tavern.com. $–$$. No Metro Access. Cabs Available on Wisconsin Ave.* ●

National Air & Space Museum

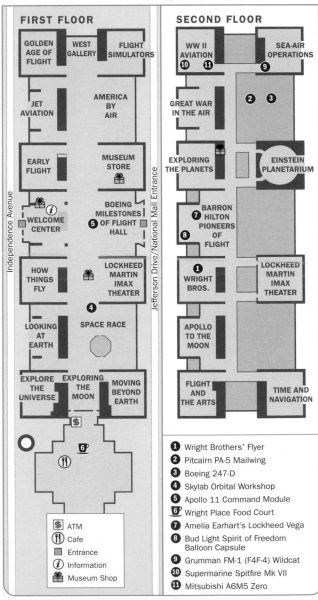

FIRST FLOOR

GOLDEN AGE OF FLIGHT

WEST GALLERY

FLIGHT SIMULATORS

JET AVIATION

AMERICA BY AIR

EARLY FLIGHT

MUSEUM STORE 🎁

WELCOME CENTER ⓘ 🎁

BOEING MILESTONES OF FLIGHT HALL ❺

HOW THINGS FLY

LOCKHEED MARTIN IMAX THEATER 🎁

❹

LOOKING AT EARTH

SPACE RACE

EXPLORE THE UNIVERSE

EXPLORING THE MOON

MOVING BEYOND EARTH

$

☕ 6

🍴

Independence Avenue

Jefferson Drive/National Mall Entrance

SECOND FLOOR

WW II AVIATION ❿ ⓫

SEA-AIR OPERATIONS ❾

GREAT WAR IN THE AIR

❷ ❸

EXPLORING THE PLANETS

EINSTEIN PLANETARIUM

BARRON HILTON PIONEERS OF FLIGHT ❼ ❽

WRIGHT BROS. ❶

LOCKHEED MARTIN IMAX THEATER

APOLLO TO THE MOON

FLIGHT AND THE ARTS

TIME AND NAVIGATION

❶ Wright Brothers' Flyer
❷ Pitcairn PA-5 Mailwing
❸ Boeing 247-D
❹ Skylab Orbital Workshop
❺ Apollo 11 Command Module
6 Wright Place Food Court
❼ Amelia Earhart's Lockheed Vega
❽ Bud Light Spirit of Freedom Balloon Capsule
❾ Grumman FM-1 (F4F-4) Wildcat
❿ Supermarine Spitfire Mk VII
⓫ Mitsubishi A6M5 Zero

$ ATM
🍴 Cafe
⬛ Entrance
ⓘ Information
🎁 Museum Shop

Previous Page: Boeing Milestones of Flight Hall at the National Air & Space Museum.

Maybe you fantasize about soaring high above the clouds, visiting galaxies far, far away, or traveling in spaceships to distant planets. Since it opened in 1976, the National Air and Space Museum has been one of the most visited museums on the National Mall. It's also one of the largest, holding some 30,000 aviation artifacts and 9,000 space artifacts ranging from the Wright Brothers' 1903 Flyer to passenger jetliners, rockets, lunar rocks, and spacesuits. It also houses the Lockheed Martin IMAX Theater, where you can tour the galaxies from the safety of your seat. The following itinerary features hallmarks of the collection. Plan to spend a couple of hours here; avionics lovers may want to linger an afternoon or a day. START: **Metro to L'Enfant Plaza.**

❶ Wright Brother's Flyer (1903). Wilbur and Orville Wright pioneered early flight after building and testing several piloted gliders and kites. Then, on Dec. 17, 1903, this aircraft—the first powered airplane with a propulsion system—took off in Kitty Hawk, N.C., for a 12-second flight, traveling 120 ft. The brothers made three more flights with the plane that day, until a large gust of wind overturned the plane. It was never flown again, but on that day, modern aviation was born. *Early Flight, first floor.*

❷ Pitcairn PA-5 Mailwing (1927). FedEx it was not, but this little plane, one of the first air mail carriers, flew the East Coast corridor extensively, carrying mail between Philadelphia, Baltimore, Washington, Richmond, and Atlanta. The 760-mile route was flown in 7 hours, just one-third the time it took by rail. The mail was carried in a fireproof metal-lined compartment forward of the pilot's cockpit. The U.S. Airmail service flew the Mailwing fleet extensively from 1927, until more efficient planes and heavier mail loads eventually rendered them obsolete. *America by Air, first floor.*

❸ Boeing 247-D (1934). Passenger air travel took a giant leap forward with the introduction of the Boeing 247-D in 1933. The plane held 10 passengers and three crew members, and offered a low

The Pitcairn PA-5 Mailwing was designed to carry airmail in the eastern United States.

Practical Matters

The National Air and Space Museum (☎ 202/633-2214; www.airandspace.si.edu) is on the south side of The Mall, between the U.S. Capitol and the Smithsonian Castle. It is at Independence Avenue and 6th St., SW. Admission is free. The museum is open daily from 10am to 5:30pm, except December 25.

vibration level, plush seats, and, for the first time, cabin air conditioning. It was also 50 percent faster than its competitors, reducing the journey from San Francisco to New York to 19 1/2 hours, compared to the previous 27-hour air travel time. *America by Air, first floor.*

❹ Skylab Orbital Workshop (1973). Before the International Space Station and Russia's Mir, there was Skylab, America's first space station. This backup to the Skylab, which orbited Earth from 1973 to 1979, is on view and open to museum-goers. It houses the living quarters, work and storage areas, and research equipment for a three-person crew to spend up to 84 days in space. *Space Race, first floor. Entrance to Skylab, second floor.*

Apollo 11 Command Module.

❺ Apollo 11 Command Module (1969). Neil Armstrong, Edwin "Buzz" Aldrin and Michael Collins lived aboard this command module, dubbed the "Columbia," during most of the first manned lunar landing mission in July 1969. Neither the Service Module or the Lunar Module ("Eagle"), which Aldrin and Armstrong used to descend to the Moon's surface, returned to Earth. *Space Race, first floor.*

☕ Wright Place Food Court. Rest your feet and nosh on food from McDonald's, Boston Market, or Donatos Pizzeria. No phone. First floor. $

❼ Amelia Earhart's Lockheed Vega (1927). Amelia Earhart flew this plane, nicknamed the "Little

Supermarine Spitfire Mk. VII.

Red Bus," alone nonstop across the Atlantic Ocean in 1930 and then nonstop across the U.S. from Los Angeles to Newark, N.J. The flights, both firsts for a woman, instantly made Earhart a worldwide sensation. *Barron Hilton Pioneers of Flight, second floor.*

❽ Bud Light Spirit of Freedom Balloon Capsule (2002). Adventurer Steve Fossett became the first person to make a solo flight around the world in a balloon when he launched this one from Northam, Australia, on June 19, 2002. During the trip he reached speeds of up to 204 miles per hour and flew as high as 34,700 feet. Fossett landed in Queensland, Australia, 14 days and 19 hours after he took off. *Barron Hilton Pioneers of Flight, second floor.*

❾ Grumman FM-1 (F4F-4) Wildcat (1940). Following Pearl Harbor, the F4F Wildcat was the primary fighter aircraft operated by the United States Navy and the Marine Corps. Its small size, folding wings and modest weight made it a favorite among convoy escort carriers. During the defense of Wake Island in World War II, American Wildcat pilots broke up many Japanese air attacks and sank a cruiser and a submarine. *Sea-Air Operations, second floor.*

❿ Supermarine Spitfire Mk VII (1938). This fast, maneuverable plane saw service on every major front during World War II. A legend in British air history, the plane was also employed by the French, Belgians, Poles and Americans during the war. While its speed and firepower made it a fierce fighter, it was also involved in several sea-air rescue operations, dropping dinghies and supplies to downed pilots. *World War II Aviation, second floor.*

⓫ Mitsubishi A6M5 Zero (1943). One of the lightest and deadliest planes in World War II history, this fighter was flown by Japanese naval aviators during the attacks on Pearl Harbor and in the Philippines. The "Zeroes" proved to be incredibly tough during close combat "dog-fighting," often outmaneuvering American fighters. The plane on display came from a group of 12 Japanese aircraft captured on Saipan Island in April 1944. *World War II Aviation, second floor.*

Museum of **Natural History**

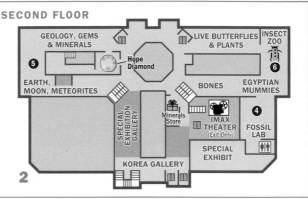

SECOND FLOOR

GEOLOGY, GEMS & MINERALS

Hope Diamond

5

EARTH, MOON, METEORITES

LIVE BUTTERFLIES & PLANTS

INSECT ZOO

6

BONES

EGYPTIAN MUMMIES

SPECIAL EXHIBITION GALLERY

Minerals Store

IMAX THEATER *(Exit Only)*

4

FOSSIL LAB

SPECIAL EXHIBIT

KOREA GALLERY

2

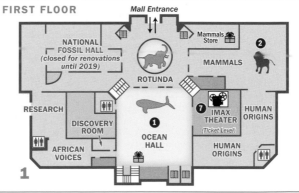

FIRST FLOOR

Mall Entrance

NATIONAL FOSSIL HALL *(closed for renovations until 2019)*

Mammals Store

2

MAMMALS

ROTUNDA

RESEARCH

DISCOVERY ROOM

1

OCEAN HALL

7

IMAX THEATER *(Ticket Level)*

HUMAN ORIGINS

AFRICAN VOICES

HUMAN ORIGINS

1

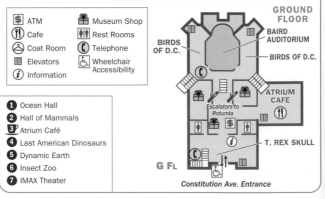

💲 ATM	🏛 Museum Shop
🍴 Cafe	🚻 Rest Rooms
⬣ Coat Room	📞 Telephone
▦ Elevators	♿ Wheelchair Accessibility
ⓘ Information	

GROUND FLOOR

BIRDS OF D.C.

BAIRD AUDITORIUM

BIRDS OF D.C.

Escalators to Rotunda

ATRIUM CAFE

T. REX SKULL

G FL

Constitution Ave. Entrance

1 Ocean Hall
2 Hall of Mammals
3 Atrium Café
4 Last American Dinosaurs
5 Dynamic Earth
6 Insect Zoo
7 IMAX Theater

Kids go ape over this museum, "dedicated to understanding the natural world and our place in it." This vast repository houses thousands of natural relics, some of which date back millions of years. If you care to learn about global warming, African cultures, the social habits of insects, the Big Bang, or fossilized bones, you might end up wishing you'd devoted your entire trip to the largest of the Smithsonian Institution's 14 museums. Of the Smithsonian's 142 million objects, nearly 90%—that's 125 million artifacts—belong to this museum. Give yourself an hour at a minimum to explore this place. START: **Metro to Archives, Judiciary Square, or Smithsonian**

Ocean Hall.

❶ Ocean Hall. Head first to this 23,000-square-foot (2,044-sq.-m) hall, the largest, most diverse exhibit of its kind in the world. Designed by the same firm that created the exhibits and spaces of the highly interactive International Spy Museum, the hall includes collections and state-of-the-art technology to demonstrate our oceans' essential role in life on earth. Look for ice age animals and loads of fossilized plants, among other preserved treasures. A model of a 45-foot-long (14m) North Atlantic right whale and the remains of a giant squid measuring 25-feet-long are also big hits. *First floor.*

❷ Hall of Mammals. Set in the restored west wing, with up-to-date lighting and sound, this exhibit features interactive dioramas that explain how mammals evolved and adapted to changes in habitat and climate over millions of years. More than 270 stuffed mammals, including a polar bear and a lion, are on display, along with a dozen mammal fossils. From time to time, the hall erupts with animal sounds, all part of the curatorial wizardry that helps make your visit a lifelike experience. *First floor.*

A 14-foot tall African elephant greets visitors in the lobby of the National Museum of Natural History.

3 **Atrium Café.** Before heading up to the second floor, make a pit stop for a quick sandwich, snack, or even a cold one. *No phone. Ground Floor. $.*

4 ★★ **The Last American Dinosaurs.** The museum's famed National Fossil Hall is undergoing

Get up close and personal with creepy-crawlies at the Insect Zoo.

renovations until 2019, but gallery goers can still get up close and personal with the real Jurassic Park in the museum's "The Last American Dinosaur" exhibition. Larger-than-life fossilized skeletons of Triceratops and Tyrannosaurus rex dominate the display, which also includes dozens of smaller animal and plant specimens, touchable samples, and a focus on modern extinctions including the dodo bird and flightless moa. Chat with museum staff and volunteers in the Fossil Lab (within the exhibit) as they unpack new fossil shipments from the field, prepare fossils for examination and help conserve those precious rocks. *Second floor.*

5 ★★★ **The Dynamic Earth.** This exhibition features the famous, cursed Hope Diamond. Legend has it that the rare blue diamond was originally stolen in the late 17th century, in its native India, from a statue of the Hindu goddess Sita. Following the incident, the object reputedly brought bad luck to anyone who claimed it. From nasty French royals Louis XVI and Marie

Practical Matters

The National Museum of Natural History (☎ 202/633-1000; www.mnh.si.edu) is on the north side of The Mall, on Constitution Avenue NW, between 9th and 10th streets. Admission is free. The museum is open daily from 10am to 5:30pm (until 7:30pm in summer; call ahead to confirm), except December 25.

Antoinette to a consortium of wealthy playboys and socialites, all either met untimely deaths or watched their dearest loved ones die badly—very badly. Jeweler Harry Winston purchased the gem in 1958 and immediately gave it to the museum, probably with more than a little relief. Here you can also learn all you want about earth science, from volcanology to the importance of mining. Interactive computers, animated graphics, and a multimedia presentation of the "big picture" story of the earth are among the features that have advanced the exhibit and the museum a bit farther into the 21st century. *Second floor.*

❻ ★ Insect Zoo. Those with an interest in creepy-crawlies can view live spiders, ants, millipedes, and centipedes up close, and learn what made the arthropods the animal kingdom's biggest grouping. Kids enjoy looking at tarantulas, centipedes, and the like, and crawling through a model of an African termite mound. *Second floor.*

❼ IMAX Theater. You just might jump out of your seat as nature's untamed beasts come barreling at you. Whether you are exploring the aliens of the deep oceans, taking a wild safari, or visiting Harry Potter's Hogwarts School of Wizardry, here you'll find the wonders of the world (and supernatural world) up close and at their most thrilling. Films rotate regularly; check the website to see what's playing during your visit. *First floor.*

While the Fossil Hall is being renovated you can see dinosaur skeletons at the "Last American Dinosaur" exhibit.

Museum of American History

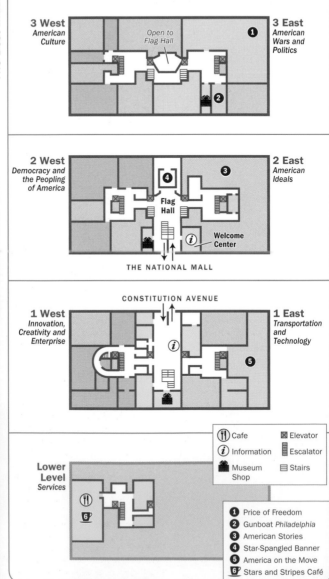

3 West
American Culture

Open to Flag Hall

3 East
American Wars and Politics

❶

❷

2 West
Democracy and the Peopling of America

Flag Hall

❹

❸

2 East
American Ideals

(i) Welcome Center

THE NATIONAL MALL

CONSTITUTION AVENUE

1 West
Innovation, Creativity and Enterprise

(i)

1 East
Transportation and Technology

❺

Lower Level
Services

🍴

6☕

🍴 Cafe	⊠ Elevator
(i) Information	▤ Escalator
🎁 Museum Shop	⊟ Stairs

❶ Price of Freedom
❷ Gunboat *Philadelphia*
❸ American Stories
❹ Star-Spangled Banner
❺ America on the Move
6☕ Stars and Stripes Café

Calling all pop culture fans and American history buffs: This seriously entertaining Smithsonian museum is home to more than three million national treasures. Check out Dizzy Gillespie's angled trumpet, Dorothy's ruby red slippers, Julia Childs' kitchen, and Muhammad Ali's boxing gloves. The original flag that inspired the national anthem is here, too, housed in a new high-tech gallery dedicated to its preservation. Plan to spend a few hours soaking up your fill of good ole Americana. START: **Metro to Smithsonian**

❶ ★★ Political History.

Throughout the museum, you'll find tons of artifacts, documents, and photographs celebrating the nation's political and presidential greats. The collection ranges from election campaign posters and ballots, to first ladies' clothing, to the personal effects of George Washington, Thomas Jefferson and Abraham Lincoln. You'll see the top hat Lincoln wore on April 14, 1865, the night he was shot at Ford's Theatre; the cloth banner honoring the electoral victory of Thomas Jefferson over John Adams in 1800; and a Civil War surgical set. You'll also see more recent artifacts, such as a piece of the World Trade Center recovered after the September 11, 2001 terrorist attacks.

USS Gunboat Philadelphia.

Dorothy's ruby red slippers, at the National Museum of American History.

❷ Gunboat *Philadelphia.* The

only surviving gunboat from the Revolutionary War, the *Philadelphia* is one of eight identical ships constructed in the 1770s. It measures 53 feet (16m) long and 15 feet (4.5m) wide and was mounted with two cannons and numerous swivel guns. The *Philadelphia* was sunk in battle by the British in New York's Lake Champlain, and remained at the bottom of Valcour Bay until 1935 when historians recovered it. The cold waters had kept its wood intact all those years, and it now rests here, along with the 24-pound (11kg) English cannonball that sent it to the bottom over 200 years ago.

Practical Matters

The National Museum of American History (☎ 202/633-1000, www.americanhistory.si.edu) is located on the National Mall at 14th St. Admission is free. The museum is open daily 10am–5:30pm (until 7:30pm on select days); closed December 25.

❸ ★★★ **Music, Sports, and Entertainment History.** Pop culture icons and other mainstays get a front-row seat at this museum. Even non-Hollywood buffs will appreciate X-files memorabilia, Bruce Willis' T-shirts from Die Hard (he donated them to the museum in 2007), Archie Bunker's armchair from the popular (and controversial) sitcom *All in the Family*, the original Kermit the Frog puppet, and a Dumbo the Flying Elephant Car Ride from 1955 Disneyland. A 1923 Yankee Stadium ticket booth, a 1989 Nintendo Gameboy, Julia Child's entire kitchen from her Cambridge, Massachusetts, home—donated part-and-parcel by the cook in 2001 when she moved residences—and the R2-D2 and

Kermit the Frog puppet from 1970.

C-3PO robots from the 1983 George Lucas blockbuster *Return of the Jedi* are just some of the favorites found in this museum's vast collection.

❹ ★★★ **The Star-Spangled Banner.** The British bombardment of Baltimore's Fort McHenry on September 14, 1814, lasted 25 hours, but at its conclusion, this "flag was still there." The poignant sight of its battle-weary stripes and stars inspired Francis Scott Key to write *The Defence of Fort McHenry*, a poem that would eventually become the nation's National Anthem, titled *The Star-Spangled Banner.* The Smithsonian acquired the flag in 1907, and it has been undergoing restoration at the museum ever since. The exhibit is an integral part to the museum and the nearly 200-year-old flag is now housed in a new, interactive gallery. The temperature and lighting of the special chamber in which it lies are regulated to protect the 30-by-34 foot (9 x 10m) flag from any more wear and tear, and the multi-story gallery with floor-to-ceiling glass windows is designed to give visitors a sense of the same "dawn's early light" that Key observed that morning in the harbor near Fort McHenry. The surrounding installation chronicles the story behind the flag's missing pieces, the Smithsonian's preservation efforts, and the national history that this artifact represents.

Julia Child donated her entire kitchen to the Smithsonian when she moved out of her Cambridge, Massachusetts home.

❺ ★ America on the Move.

Do you still reminiscence about your first muscle car? It's likely represented here, along with a Chicago Transit Authority car, a 1903 Winton (the first car driven across the U.S.), a 92-foot-long (28m) Southern Railway locomotive, and even 40 feet (18m) of the American Southwest's renowned Route 66. Motor on down to the ground floor of the museum to see the nearly 20 life-size dioramas depicting America's transit history, from the first covered wagons that braved the Wild West to motor vehicles whose brethren still ply Route 66 and I-95 today. A range of some 300 artifacts—including railway markers, signs, and photographs—are displayed in period settings to illustrate the story of how America's railroad, canals, and roads changed the way its people traveled.

Southern Railway Locomotive in the "America on the Move" exhibit.

❻ Stars and Stripes Café.

Head to this aptly named cafe on the lower level for a culinary slice of Americana: basic soups, salads, burgers, pizzas, and desserts. *No phone.* $–$$.

19th- & 20th-Century Art
Museums

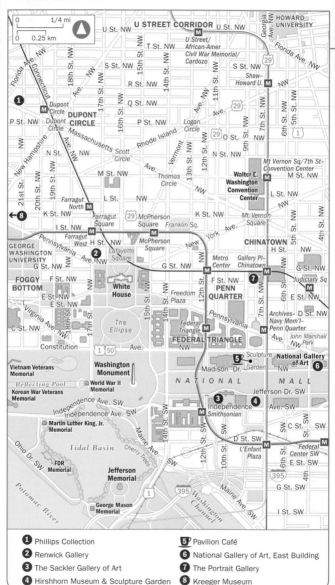

1. Phillips Collection
2. Renwick Gallery
3. The Sackler Gallery of Art
4. Hirshhorn Museum & Sculpture Garden
5. Pavilion Café
6. National Gallery of Art, East Building
7. The Portrait Gallery
8. Kreeger Museum

I n a world where what's considered current changes at an ever-faster pace—"That's, like, so 30 seconds ago!"—it's refreshing to view the art of the 1800s and 1900s, still thought of as modern, if not so subversive, well into the 21st century. It's also fun to put those art history classes to the test. START: **Metro to Dupont Circle (Q St. exit).**

1 Phillips Collection. The building that houses the Phillips Collection, which is widely considered America's first museum of modern art, was once the home of Duncan Phillips, grandson of the cofounder of the Jones and Laughlin Steel Company. The modern-looking newer wing generally shows fresh exhibitions; the museum also plays host to special lectures and tours. Some of its 2,472 artworks include Pierre-Auguste Renoir's *Luncheon of the Boating Party* (1880–81), Vincent van Gogh's *The Road Menders* (1889), Edgar Degas's *Dancers at the Barre* (1900), and Georges Rouault's *Christ & the High Priest* (1937). ⏱ *1 hr. 1600 21st St. NW.* ☎ *202/387-2151. www.phillips collection.org. Adults $12; students and seniors $10; 18 and under free. Tues–Sat 10am–5pm (Thurs to 5:30pm); Sun noon–7pm (June– Sept to 5pm).*

2 The Renwick Gallery. Newly reopened after a major 2-year renovation, the Renwick houses the Smithsonian's American Art Museum's collection of contemporary craft and decorative arts. Edgy and creative modern artwork abounds here, including Andy Paiko's *Spinning Wheel* (2007), and Lino Tagliapietra's *Mandara* (2005), made of intricate, colorful glass. Revolving special exhibitions featuring modern artists are also on view. ⏱ *1 hr. Pennsylvania Avenue at 17th Street NW. 202/633-7970. www.renwick. americanart.si.edu. Free admission. Daily 10am–5:30pm, except Dec. 25.*

"Wonder" exhibit in Renwick Gallery.

3 The Sackler Gallery of Art. The Smithsonian Institution has two museums dedicated to Asian art: the Freer Gallery of Art and the Arthur M. Sackler Gallery. While the Freer undergoes major renovations (it will reopen in 2017), the adjacent Sackler features both permanent and temporary exhibitions, combining some of the two collections, and continues to host contemporary Asian art. Highlights include South Asian sculpture, Chinese jades and bronzes, and modern Japanese ceramics. Many of the paintings by American artist James McNeill Whistler, previously housed at the Freer, will also be on view at the Sackler during renovation. ⏱ *1 hr. 1050 Independence Avenue,*

SW ☎ 202/633-4880. www.asia.si.edu. Free admission. Daily 10am–5:30pm, except Dec 25.

❹ ★ Hirshhorn Museum & Sculpture Garden. First opened in 1974, the Hirshhorn Museum—built 14 feet (4.2m) above ground on sculptured supports—is a unique vessel for a singular collection of modern and contemporary art. Amassed around Latvian émigré Joseph Hirshhorn's original donation of more than 9,500 works to the United States, the collection now includes works by Christo, Joseph Cornell, Arshile Gorky, and others. In the outdoor Plaza, visitors can gawk at the giant fountain and surreal sculptures. The Hirshhorn also has a sculpture garden across the street, with some 60 works of art. Other highlights of this eclectic outdoor exhibition are Emile-Antonine Bourdelle's *Great Warrior of Montauban* (1898–1900, cast 1956); Alexander Calder's *Stabile-Mobile (Red Lily)*, 1947); Edward Hopper's *City Sunlight* (1954); Edgar Degas' *Dancer Putting on Stocking* (1896); Rodin's *The Burghers of Calais* (1884–89); and Alberto Giacometti's *Standing Woman I* (1961). ⏱ *1 hr. Independence Ave. at 7th St. NW.* ☎ 202/633-4674. www.hirshhorn.org. *Free admission. Daily*

10am–5:30pm; plaza 7:30am–5:30pm, except Dec 25; sculpture garden 7:30am–dusk.

5️⃣ Pavilion Café. This cafeteria-style lunch spot serves salads, veggie wraps, grilled meats, sandwiches, pizza, espresso drinks, and yummy baked goods, near the National Gallery of Art Sculpture Garden. Dine outdoors on warm days, or admire the ice-skating rink on cold ones, from inside the cafe's family-friendly environs. *9th St. and Constitution Ave. NW (near Sculpture Garden).* ☎ 202/289-3360. $

❻ ★★★ National Gallery of Art, East Building. The trademarks of this 1978 I. M. Pei–designed building are its adjoining triangles, in pink Tennessee marble (from the same quarry as the neoclassical West Wing), that form sharp, acute angles at the corners. Inside, the centerpiece is the 76-foot-long (23m), 920-pound (417kg) mobile by Alexander Calder, which hangs from the ceiling of the main atrium. The mobile's construction includes aluminum tubing and aluminum honeycomb panels, which allow its arms to slowly and gracefully rotate. With 295 paintings and

Hirshhorn Museum & Sculpture Garden.

more than 650 sketches, the National Gallery has one of the largest collections of Mark Rothko artwork in the world. The East Building is also home to works by Jackson Pollock, Pablo Picasso, Georgia O'Keefe, and Alberto Giacometti. ⓘ *1 hr. At press time, the East Building was closed for renovations. Check the web site for details on where to find specific works following its reopening. The National Mall, between 3rd and 7th sts.* ☎ *202/737-4215. www.nga.gov. Free admission. Mon–Sat 10am–5pm; Sun 11am–6pm; closed Dec 25 and Jan 1.*

❼ The National Portrait Gallery. Portraits of noteworthy Americans, from Rosa Parks to George Gershwin, and American pop culture icons, such as Babe Ruth and Marilyn Monroe, can be found at this museum, set in one of Washington's oldest buildings. The museum also has one of the nation's only complete collections of presidential portraits outside the White House, including Gilbert Stuart's famous painting of George Washington. Don't miss the Kogod Courtyard with its surreal,

"floating" glass ceiling. ⓘ *1 hr. 8th and F sts. NW.* ☎ *202/633-8300. www.npg.si.edu. Free admission. Daily 11:30am–7pm, except Dec. 25.*

❽ Kreeger Museum. This private museum is housed in the former residence of David and Carmen Kreeger, well-known collectors who amassed a sizable holding of 19th- and 20th-century paintings and sculptures. Highlights include works by Monet, van Gogh, Pissarro, Rodin, Kandinksy, and Cezanne. As you tour the museum, take note of its modern architecture. Designed by architect Philip Johnson, it features a steel and concrete frame with glass walls and a free-form design. ⓘ *2 hr. including commute. 2401 Foxhall Rd., NW;* ☎ *202/337-3050, ext. 10. Tour reservations required:* ☎ *202/338-3552. Adults, $10; students (with ID) and seniors over 65, $7; 12 and under, free. Tues–Thurs: Museum open only for tours at 10:30am and 1:30pm. Reservations required. Fri–Sat 10am–4pm, no reservations needed. Sculpture garden: Tues–Sat 10am–4pm. www.kreegermuseum.org. No Metro access*

Special-Interest Museums

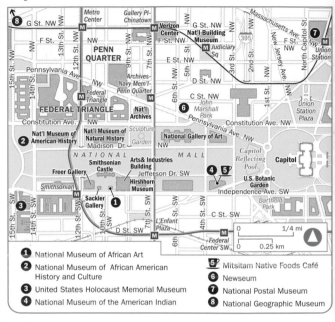

1. National Museum of African Art
2. National Museum of African American History and Culture
3. United States Holocaust Memorial Museum
4. National Museum of the American Indian
5. Mitsitam Native Foods Café
6. Newseum
7. National Postal Museum
8. National Geographic Museum

Maybe you fantasize about grabbing the microphone and taking a spin on camera as a news anchor. Perhaps you want to learn more about a particular ethnic group's art, culture, and storied history. Whatever your inclination may be, Washington can satisfy it, as home to many renowned special-interest museums. Here are a few of distinction. START: **Metro to L'Enfant Plaza or Smithsonian.**

① National Museum of African Art. The only national museum solely dedicated to the acquisition, study, and exhibition of African art, this collection features both traditional and contemporary pieces, including everything from the spiritual (a Koranic writing board from Nigeria, an ivory pendant from the Congo) to the beautiful but practical (a carved wood fly whisk handle from Cote d'Ivoire). Ongoing exhibits include one focusing on African textiles: woven tapestries, robes, and clothes with

particularly notable decorations and designs. Another exhibit features more than 130 contemporary and traditional art works from the continent. The museum also features regular music programs and tours. ⏱ 1 hr. 950 Independence Ave. NW. ☎ 202/633-4600. www. africa.si.edu. Free admission. Daily 10am–5:30pm, except Dec 25.

② National Museum of African American History and Culture. The newest museum to the National Mall spotlights the African

Bowl with Figures from Nigeria by Olowe of Ise.

American experience through its history and culture. The museum's collection spans the era of slavery, the period of Reconstruction, the Harlem Renaissance, and the civil rights movement, and ranges from works of art to photographs, archival documents, electronic data, and audio recordings. At press time the museum was still under construction, with plans to open in fall 2016. In the meantime, there's a temporary exhibit on view at the National Museum of American History. ⏱ 1 hr. *Constitution Avenue between 14th and 15th sts NW.* ☎ *202/633-4600. www.nmaahc.si.edu. Free admission. Daily 10am–5:30pm, except Dec 25.*

❸ ★★ **United States Holocaust Memorial Museum.** Be prepared to take an emotional journey when you enter this space, a living memorial to "never forgetting" the genocide of Europe's Jews, and the murder of all who opposed the rise of Germany's Nazi party, before and during World War II. Upon entering, you will be given (to keep) a faux passport of an actual Holocaust victim; some survived, but the great majority did not. The museum's centerpiece is its three-floor exhibit, entitled "The Holocaust." It's broken up into three subsections: "Nazi Assault," "Final Solution," and "Last Chapter." Through hundreds of artifacts and film footage, the story of one of humankind's biggest tragedies is laid out in exhaustive detail. The museum recommends that visitors be 11 years of age or older, due to the intensity of the material. There is also a museum shop, a cafe, and the Wexner Learning Center on the second floor, where visitors can explore the survivors' registry and view materials about topics such as the Nuremberg Trials. ⏱ *1hr. 100 Raoul Wallenberg Place SW.* ☎ *202/488-044. www.ushmm.org. Free admission, but timed passes are necessary for visiting the permanent exhibition, and can be obtained at the museum on the day of your visit or in advance by calling Tickets.com (☎ 800/400–9373). Each day, the museum distributes a large but limited number of timed-entry passes, on a first-come, first-served basis, for use that same day. Daily 10am–5:30pm, except Yom Kippur and Dec 25.*

❹ ★★ **National Museum of the American Indian.** It's one of the most distinctive museums on the National Mall, with exterior walls that are organically curved to suggest rock worn down by water. Dedicated to preserving the culture and history of Native Americans, the museum is also one of the most technologically advanced: Exhibits routinely incorporate video and other multimedia, including "Our Lives," which shows how Native American tribes live in contemporary times while striving to keep their ethnic identity. ⏱ *1hr. 4th St. and Independence Ave. NW.* ☎ *202/633-1000. www.nmai.si.edu. Free admission. Daily 10am–5:30pm, except Dec 25.*

5 **Mitsitam Native Foods Café.** On the American Indian museum's first floor, you can sample meals based on traditional Native American cuisines. *No phone. $–$$.*

6 ★★★ **Newseum.** The history of news is told through interactive games and close-up views of hundreds of publications. Hear first-person accounts from reporters in the field, see a comprehensive collection of Pulitzer-Prize winning photojournalists' images, and discover the secrets to electronic news reporting. The "Be a Reporter" exhibit puts visitors in the hot seat: With a deadline looming and a breaking news story to report, grab a microphone and test your skills in front of the camera. How would you fare as the next Walter Cronkite? ⏱ *2 hr. 555 Pennsylvania Ave. NW.* ☎ *202/292-6100. www.newseum. org Daily 9am–5pm, except Thanksgiving, Dec 25, and Jan 1. Adults,*

$23, seniors, $19, kids 7–18, $14, children 6 and under free. Metro: Archives/Navy Memorial.

7 **National Postal Museum.** One of the world's largest stamp collections resides at this ode to the U.S. Mail Service, established in 1886. Listen to tales of the early Pony Express and browse a vast assortment of historical postage dating back to the nation's infancy, plus international stamps, the first piece of correspondence to be flown across the Atlantic, and some original 24-cent inverted stamps. ⏱ *1 hr. 2 Massachusetts Ave. NE.* ☎ *202/633-5555. www.postalmuseum.si.edu. Free admission. Daily 10am–5:30pm, except Dec 25. Metro: Union Station.*

8 **National Geographic Museum.** Fans of the magazine and kids of all ages will love this museum's interactive experiences, which highlight different species and cultures around the world. ⏱ *1 hr.1145 17th St., NW (at M St. NW) 202/857-7700. http://events.nationalgeographic.com/national-geographic-museum. Adults $15; seniors and students $12; kids 5–12 $10, children 4 and under free. Daily 10am–6pm.* ●

The National Museum of the American Indian.

Adams Morgan

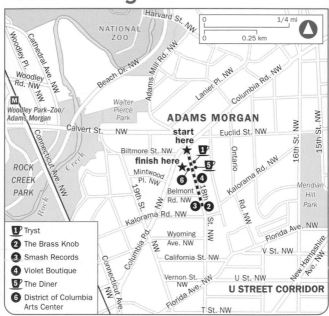

1. Tryst
2. The Brass Knob
3. Smash Records
4. Violet Boutique
5. The Diner
6. District of Columbia Arts Center

If you love New York's East Village, you'll feel right at home in this neighborhood, which is all about youthful verve, bohemian values, diversity, and a thriving street scene. Concentrate your explorations on 18th Street and the intersecting Columbia Avenue, where you'll discover authentic ethnic restaurants, girlie boutiques, funky lounges, coffeehouses with sidewalk seating, and young people on display in their various rebellious uniforms. START: **Metro to Woodley Park–Zoo/Adams Morgan.**

1 ★★ **Tryst** is one of those coffeehouses whose regulars seem to live in the place—you almost expect to find Ross, Rachel, Joey, and the gang camped out in the corner. A bar, a lounge, a diner, and a cafe, it shelters students doing homework; writers on laptops; artists hanging artwork for sale; and

mohawked 8-year-olds running around, pastries in hand. Opens very early, closes very late. *See p 149.*

2 **The Brass Knob.** Looking for vintage decorative wares or the perfect stained-glass accent for your home? Look no further than

Festival in Adams Morgan.

Sat 11am–8pm; Sun 11am–6pm. Closed Mon. Metro: Woodley Park-Zoo/Adams Morgan.

⑤ **The Diner** purports to offer something for everyone, and it lives up to this claim with a full menu of salads, sandwiches, all-day break-fast, and some of the best milk-shakes in the city. You'll feel recharged after visiting this casual neighborhood fixture in the heart of Adams Morgan. *2453 18th St. NW. ☎ 202/232-8800. www.dinerdc. com.*

this funky shop featuring one-of-a-kind objects from the 1800s to the early 1900s. You'll need plenty of time to peruse the store, filled with items such as antique chandeliers, iron gates, and, true to the shop's name, doorknobs. ⏲ *30 min. 2311 18th St. NW. ☎ 202/644-8289. www.thebrassknob.com. Mon–Sat 10:30am–6pm; Sun noon–5pm. Metro: Woodley Park-Zoo/Adams Morgan.*

⑥ **District of Columbia Arts Center.** Adams Morgan is one of D.C.'s most eclectic neighbor-hoods, so where else would you find a funky art gallery and 50-seat theater among bars and restaurants that cater to the college scene? The nonprofit DCAC features up-and-coming artists in an intimate theater space, while the 800-sq.-foot gallery spotlights a revolving calendar of innovative works. ⏲ *1½ hr. 2438 18th St. NW. ☎ 202/462-7833. www.dcartscenter.org. Wed–Sun 2–7pm. Metro: Woodley Park-Zoo/Adams Morgan.*

Shopping for antiques at The Brass Knob

❸ **Smash Records.** Spend an hour perusing the vinyl records, vin-tage clothing, and punk-rock CDs found in this hole-in-the-wall shop in the heart of Adams Morgan. If you love records, you won't leave empty-handed. ⏲ *30 min. 2314 18th St. NW, 2nd Floor. ☎ 202/38-SMASH (76274). www.smashrecords. com. Mon–Thurs noon–9pm; Fri–Sat noon–9:30pm; Sun noon–7pm. Metro: Woodley Park-Zoo/Adams Morgan.*

❹ **Violet Boutique.** A variety of affordable styles and accessories, plus super-friendly and knowledge-able owner Julie Egermayer, have made this funky shop on the main drag of Adams Morgan a go-to for fashionistas. ⏲ *30 min. 2439 18th St. NW. ☎ 202/621-9225. www. violetdc.com. Tues–Fri noon–8pm;*

U Street Corridor/14th Street

- 1 Commissary DC
- 2 Buffalo Exchange
- 3 The Galleries on 14th Street
- 4 Miss Pixie's
- 5 Home Rule
- 6 Greater U Street Heritage Trail
- 7 Lincoln Theatre
- 8 Ben's Chili Bowl
- 9 African American Civil War Memorial and Museum
- 10 Howard University

The riots of 1968—ignited by the assassination of Martin Luther King Jr.—subjected the Corridor to 3 days of looting and devastation. Once known as the grand and glorious "Black Broadway," the strip was a shadow of its former self for decades afterward, better known for its crack houses than for its theater companies. Fourteenth Street, which intersects historic U Street and runs north to south, was also decimated during the riots. But new signs of life appeared late in the 1990s in both of these areas: A frenzied real-estate boom brought homesteaders to the neighborhood and the requisite art galleries, trendsetting boutiques, scene-making cafes, and happening restaurants followed. This itinerary is a good pick if you want to sleep in a little: No early opening hours here. START: **Metro to U Street/Cardozo.**

1 Commissary DC. Kick off your day with breakfast at this cozy restaurant with outdoor tables and fantastic food served all day. The menu runs the gamut from delicious omelets to tuna melts and a fish fry. If you're lucky, snag a comfy chair up front with pullout trays. It'll feel like dining in your living room, only much better. *1443 P St. NW. (btw. N. 14th St. and N. 15th St.)* ☎ *202/299-0018. www.commissary dc.com. $$ Metro: Dupont Circle.*

② The Galleries on 14th Street. Explore D.C.'s contemporary art scene at this consortium of independent galleries: Begin your crawl at 1515 14th St. NW, which houses two talk-of-the-town galleries: Hemphill Fine Arts (☎ 202/234-5601) and Adamson Gallery (☎ 202/232-0707). Then check out Transformer (1404 P St. NW; ☎ 202/483-1102), Gallery plan b (1530 14th St. NW; ☎ 202/234-2711), and G Fine Art (4718 14th St. NW; ☎ 202/462-1601). ⏱ 2 hr. Metro: Cardozo/U St.

③ Miss Pixie's. Even if you don't think you need it, you'll still have to have it when you encounter this funky shop's eclectic collection of antiques, odd trinkets, and one-of-a-kind furniture cobbled from estate sales. The inventory rotates, so artful bookcases and retro chairs might be there one week and gone the next. ⏱ 30 min. 1626 14th St. NW. (between N. R St. & N. Corcoran St.). ☎ 202/232-8171. www.misspixies.com. Daily 11am–/pm. Metro: U Street/Cardozo

④ Home Rule. Need a milk frother, stainless steel martini shaker, or a pair of "pot-holder dogs" (oven mitts that look like

Shopping at Home Rule.

your mutt)? Of course you do! Look no further than this culinary-themed outpost for creative, colorful kitchen and bar accessories. ⏱ 30 min. 1807 14th St. NW (at S St.). ☎ 202/797-5544. www.homerule.com. Mon–Sat 11am–7pm; Sun noon–5:30pm. Closed holidays. AE, DISC, MC, V. Metro: Cardozo/U St.

⑤ Buffalo Exchange. Find everything from the current trends, designer labels, and leather to vintage and one-of-a-kind items at this unique consignment boutique, dedicated to sustainability in

Shopping at Buffalo Exchange.

Next door to Lincoln Theater, Ben's Chili Bowl is convenient for a quick bite before or after a show.

fashion. ⏱ *30 min. 1318 14th St. NW.* ☎ *202/299-9148. www.buffalo exchange.com.*

⑥ ★★ Greater U Street Heritage Trail. As you explore this section of town—the former home of Duke Ellington and the vital heart of African-American culture in the capital—keep an eye out for 14 poster-size signs, with historical images and compelling stories. Follow these visual cues, and you can take a 90-minute, self-guided tour of historic U Street. The first sign is at 13th and U streets NW, near the Cardozo/U Street/African-American Civil War Memorial Metro stop; each sign will direct you to the next. Highlights include the Thurgood Marshall Center for Service and Heritage (home to the first African-American YMCA), the Whitelaw Hotel (the segregated capital's first luxury hotel for African Americans), the revived Bohemian Caverns (where the Ramsey Lewis Trio recorded the album "In Crowd"), and the restored Lincoln Theatre (see the next stop). Walkers are encouraged to follow the trail at their own pace, sampling neighborhood character, businesses, and restaurants along the way. For more

information, a timeline of historical U Street events and vintage photographs, stop in the Greater U Street Neighborhood Visitor Center, located at the start of the trail near the Cardozo/U Street Metro stop. ⏱ *1½ hr. 1211 U St. NW.* ☎ *202/661-7581. www.culturaltourism dc.org (click on "Tours & Trails"). Daily 10am–8pm.*

⑦ ★ Lincoln Theatre. The jewel of what was once called "Black Broadway," the Lincoln hosted the likes of Ella Fitzgerald and Cab Calloway before desegregation. The theater went dark in 1979 but reopened 15 years later and was eventually restored to its original 1920s splendor. Today, it books jazz, R & B, gospel, and comedy acts—even events such as the D.C. Film Festival. ⏱ *½ hr., or more if you plan to see a show. 1215 U St. NW.* ☎ *202/888-0050. www.thelincolndc. com. Tickets $20–$200. Metro: Cardozo/U St.*

⑧ ★★ Ben's Chili Bowl. Open since 1958, this old-time diner is a Washington institution. If the walls could talk, they would speak volumes about historic figures such as

Greater U Street.

Martin Luther King, Jr., Redd Foxx, and others who've sat at the Formica tables here. You just might catch a celebrity inhaling a Chili Half-Smoke—a quarter-pound half pork/half beef smoked sausage, smothered in chili, of course—with a side of chili fries and an iced tea. Tip: Ben's is cash-only, but they have an ATM in case you get caught short. *1213 U St. NW.* ☎ *202/667-0909. www.benschili bowl.com. $.*

For sit-down dining, a bar, and expanded menu, head to **Ben's Next Door.** *1211 U St. NW.* ☎ *202/667-8880. www.bensnext door.com. $$.*

❾ ★ African American Civil War Memorial and Museum.

This museum uses photography, audiovisual presentations, and historical documents and artifacts to commemorate the estimated 228,000-plus African-American soldiers and sailors who fought, largely unheralded, in the U.S. Civil War. Unveiled in 1998, the *Spirit of Freedom* sculpture, 2 blocks away, honors the sacrifices made by black soldiers and their families during the war. Designed by Ed Hamilton, of Louisville, Kentucky, it is also the first major artwork by an African-American sculptor to reside on federal land in the capital. ⏱ *45 min. 1925 Vermont Ave. NW at U St.* ☎ *202/667-2667. www.afroamcivil war.org. Free admission. Tues–Fri 10am–6:30pm; Sat 10am–4pm; Sun noon–4pm. Metro: Cardozo/U St.*

The African American Civil War Monument.

❿ Howard University. Estab-

lished in 1867 by a charter of the U.S. Congress, this educational institution was named after General Oliver Howard, a Civil War hero and commissioner of the Freedman's Bureau, which was instrumental in providing funds for the upstart university. Howard U. has come to be a bastion for the liberal and scientific arts, attracting the nation's best and brightest African-American students, as well as other students of color, who are proud to continue the legacy of a school so involved in the civil rights movement of the 1960s. Current enrollment hovers near 11,000, with more than 7,000 undergraduates. Famous alumni include Thurgood Marshall, Debbie Allen, Sean "P. Diddy" Combs, Marlon Wayans, and Roberta Flack. ⏱ *20 min. 2400 6th St. NW.* ☎ *202/806-6100. www.howard.edu. Metro: Cardozo/U St.*

Dupont Circle

1 Kramerbooks & Afterwords Café
2 Phillips Collection
3 Woodrow Wilson House
4 Dupont Memorial Fountain
5 Circa
6 Lou Lou
7 Blue Mercury
8 Betsy Fisher
9 National Geographic Explorer's Hall
10 Teddy and the Bully Bar
11 Eighteenth Street Lounge

Capitol Hill and The Mall may represent Washington to the world, but for locals, Dupont Circle is the heart of the District—a central point for meeting, lunching, strolling, shopping, and people-watching. Famous for its gay-friendliness, it's just plain-old friendly to everyone, including visitors. Be sure to sit on a bench, rest your feet, and watch the world go by within the Circle itself, and ogle the master artworks at Duncan Phillips's private-home-turned-museum, The Phillips Collection (see below). For a nice mix of retailers, restaurants, bars, and clubs, check out Connecticut Avenue and nearby 17th Street. START: **Metro to Dupont Circle.**

1 ★★ **Kramerbooks & Afterwords Café.** Is it a restaurant? A bookstore? A coffeehouse? Open early and late (all night on weekends), it's the perfect spot to chat over lattes, browse bestsellers, grab a quick sandwich, and people-watch the Washingtonians who

flock here in droves. The outdoor tables are at a premium in good weather, and weekend brunch is a popular time to rendezvous with friends. ⏱ *1 hr. 1517 Connecticut Ave. NW.* ☎ *202/387-1400. www. kramers.com. $$.*

A Lindy hopping festival in Dupont Circle.

❷ ★★ Phillips Collection.
Before leaving Dupont Circle for points north, make a stop at the original home of renowned art collector Duncan Phillips. On opening his personal collection to the public in 1921, he established America's first modern art museum. His collection is still on view, and the museum remains one of the most popular in the District. Rooms in this historic brownstone feature works by Picasso, Degas, van Gogh, and O'Keeffe, along with several contemporary artists. Auguste Renoir's *Luncheon of the Boating Party* occupies an entire wall on the museum's second floor, and is the Phillips' most celebrated piece. ⏱ *2 hr. 1600 21st St. NW.* ☎ *202/387-2151. www.phillips collection.org. Adults $12; students and seniors, $10; 18 and under, free. Metro: Dupont Circle.*

❸ ★ Woodrow Wilson House.
Tour the former home of the 28th president, preserved as it was when he lived here during his final years in the 1920s. Docents guide visitors on hour-long tours of the Georgian Revival–style building, pointing out objects d'art, such as the French Gobelin tapestry given to Wilson by the French ambassador, and telling stories about our 28th president (such as the fact that he liked to whistle the tune "Oh You Beautiful Doll" to his beloved wife, Edith). You'll see Wilson's movie projector in the library (he was a film buff); the typical 1920s kitchen, with one of the nation's first electric refrigerators; and Wilson's office, which his family called "the dugout." Office treasures include a baseball given to him at an Army-Navy game he attended with England's George VI. Upstairs, on his bedside table, lies *Imitation of Christ,* by Thomas à Kempis. See also the "Historic Washington" tour on p 48. ⏱ *2 hr. 2340 S St. NW.* ☎ *202/387-4062.*

Sculpture at the Phillips Collection in Dupont Circle.

Woodrow Wilson's library and study.

www.woodrowwilsonhouse.org. $10 adults; $8 seniors; $5 students. Wed–Sun 10am–4pm; closed major holidays. Metro: Dupont Circle.

❹ Dupont Memorial Fountain. A trip to Dupont Circle will undoubtedly include a stroll through this urban park, from which the neighborhood radiates in all directions. A giant marble statue of three classical figures representing sea, wind, and sky anchors the circular area that attracts dog walkers, musicians, bookworms, and lunch-breakers. Designed by Daniel Chester French—sculptor of the seated

Dupont Memorial Fountain.

Abraham Lincoln at the Lincoln Memorial—and erected in 1921, it was placed on the National Register of Historic Places in 1978. ① *20 min. Connecticut Ave. and New Hampshire Ave., NW. Metro: Dupont Circle.*

5️⃣ Circa. Sit outside and watch the city go by while enjoying ravioli, mango salads and more than 20 wines by the glass. *1601 Connecticut Ave. NW. ☎ 202/667-1601. www.circaatdupont.com. $$.*

❻ Lou Lou. Need a belt for the night out? How about a new set of earrings? This charming boutique in the heart of Dupont Circle has more accessories than you'll ever need—hats, headbands, belts, scarves, jewelry, and bags—all at very reasonable prices. ① *30 min. 1601 Connecticut Ave. NW. ☎ 202/588-0027. www.loulou boutiques.com. Mon–Sat 10am–8pm; Sun 11am–6pm. $. Metro: Dupont Circle (North Exit).*

❼ Blue Mercury. This regional skincare, cosmetics, and bath shop has a beautiful clientele—women and men who can't buy enough of the store's Shu Uemera, Fresh,

Lou Lou Boutique.

Decleor, and Paula Dorp product lines. Limited spa and beauty treatments are also available. ⏱ *20 min. 1619 Connecticut Ave. NW.* ☎ *202/462-1300. www.bluemercury. com. Mon–Sat 10am–8pm; Sun noon–6pm. AE, DISC, MC, V. Metro: Dupont Circle or Farragut North.*

⑧ ★★ Betsy Fisher. In a world where so many of us can spot our own outfits on others, it's nice to find a boutique with unique, fashion-forward apparel, shoes, and accessories for women—not girls—that are modern without being trendy. A good place to grab some basic accessories, too—think belts, boots, shoes, and bags. *See p 106.*

⑨ ★★ kids National Geographic Explorer's Hall. If you, or your little ones, are a fan of world travel, space exploration, or both—or if you've been a reader of *National Geographic* all your life and simply want to see where the magazine is put together—this museum is a must-visit. Check out the society's rotating exhibits related to exploration, adventure, world cultures, and earth sciences, which incorporate interactive programs and artifacts. Conclude your expedition with a stop by the gift shop, whose ample collection of toys, gadgets, and gear will amuse your whole scouting party. ⏱ *1 hr. 17th and M sts. NW.* ☎ *202/857-7588. www.nationalgeographic.com/museum. $15 adults, $12 seniors, $10 kids (5–12). Daily 10am–6pm. Closed Dec 25. Tickets available online or in advance at 202/857-7700. Metro: Farragut North (Connecticut Ave. and L St. exit).*

⑩ Teddy and the Bully Bar. Pay tribute to Teddy Roosevelt, one of the country's most cowboy-ish presidents, at this boisterous spot known for its simple American menu of steak, chicken, cornbread, and much, much more. Mixologists serve classic cocktails with a twist, like the sazerac and "Sheeny's Rickey." *1200 19th St. NW.* ☎ *202/872-8700. www.teddyandthebullybar.com. $$.*

⑪ Eighteenth Street Lounge. This legendary bar is all about mingling, chilling to music, and posing pretty. Arrive early in the evening to rest your feet as you sip a cocktail and sit, salon-style, on a sofa, or show up late to listen to a DJ with all the beautiful people. *See p 151.*

Shoes on display in Betsy Fisher.

The Best **Neighborhood Walks**

Georgetown

1. Evermay
2. Oak Hill Cemetery
3. Montrose Park
4. Tudor Place
5. Ellarue
6. Georgetown University
7. Cady's Alley
8. Leopold's Kate
9. C&O Canal
10. Old Stone House
11. Bourbon Steak

No visit to Washington is complete without a trip to historic and hip Georgetown—which somehow manages to balance frenzied consumerism with cultural relevance. For some of the neighborhood's most visited attractions, check out "The Best of D.C. in 2 Days" on p 14. Here are a few additional points of interest, high-end restaurants, and outstanding retailers. START: **Bus no. 30, 32, 34, 35, 36, or 38B to Thomas Jefferson and M streets.**

1 ★★ Evermay. Built between 1792 and 1794, one of Georgetown's greatest mansions originally had an owner who was both eccentric and obsessed with privacy. He went so far as to advertise dire predictions (bordering on threats) in the daily papers, warning the curious of trespassing on his property. Today, frequent musical performances and other events are held at the renovated and restored mansion, owned by the S&R Foundation. ⏱ 30 min. 1623 28th St. NW. Check website for event details.

2 Oak Hill Cemetery. This historic cemetery is just a short walk uphill from the shops of Georgetown's M Street. One of the oldest cemeteries in the city, it was established in 1849 and now holds the remains of many famous Washingtonians: Senators, Civil War generals, artists, designers, and Philip Graham, longtime publisher of the *Washington Post,* are all buried here. Among the grounds' great buildings and monuments are the Van Ness Mausoleum and

Oak Hill Cemetery.

Renwick Chapel, designed by James Renwick, Jr., architect of the Smithsonian Building. ⏱ *30 min. 30th and R sts. NW.* ☎ *202/337-2835. www.oakhillcemeterydc.org. Mon–Fri, 10am–4:30pm; closed to the public on holidays and during funerals.*

❸ ★ **Montrose Park.** Right next door to Oak Hill, Montrose was founded as a place "for the recreation and pleasure of the people." Rope-making tycoon Robert Parrott claimed the land in the early 1800s, and by the early 1900s, it had become the premier spot in town for picnics and leisurely strolls. Street noises are so muffled, you might even feel you've left the city. ⏱ *45 min. On the block of 3000 R St. NW, next to Dumbarton Oaks. Open daily Mar 15–Oct 31, 2–6pm; Nov 1–Mar 14, 2–5pm.*

❹ ★ **Tudor Place.** One of the longest blocks in Georgetown is the stretch between Q and R streets on 31st Street NW. In a neighborhood where even the rich and famous get dog-eat-dog over square footage, it doesn't get more impressive than this estate, which sprawls nearly a full square block. This 1816 mansion was home to Martha Washington's granddaughter and her descendants until 1984. ⏱ *30 min. 1644 31st St. NW.* ☎ *202/965-0400. www.tudorplace. org. Admission $10 adults, $8 seniors, $3 visitors ages 5–17. Tues–Sat 10am–4pm; Sun noon–4pm.*

❺ ★ **Ella-Rue.** Not so long ago, D.C. was all about pearls and twin-sets but, thank goodness, times have changed. This boutique is where the district's trendsetters select new and consigned looks, some from high-end designers including Emilio Pucci, Marchesa, and Tory Burch; and saliva-inducing accessories, from bags to embellished earrings.

Evermay House.

The shop-lined streets of Georgetown.

6 ★★★ Georgetown University. Like Harvard, Princeton, and Brown, Georgetown University evokes images of ivy-covered buildings, historic colleges, polo-wearing students, and academic types with furrowed brows appearing from their ivory towers. The campus grounds do not disappoint, from the architecture to the soccer pitch, and make for a lovely stroll on a nice day. Because the university is in the heart of Georgetown just a hop, skip, and a jump from M Street's main drag (west of Wisconsin), the curious should not hesitate to tour it. (Look for the nearby *Exorcist* stairs, too, which were featured in a climactic scene in the 1973

Peaceful Montrose Park is a prime spot for a picnic.

horror film, and connect the campus to M St. from Prospect St.) Founded by Father John Carroll (an appointed superior of the American Mission by the pope in 1784), the school officially opened its doors for study in 1789. More than 2 centuries later, the school is a top draw for continuing education and boasts formidable alums such as President William Jefferson Clinton, and yes, the guy who wrote *The Exorcist*, William Peter Blatty. ⏱ *30 min. 37th and O sts. NW.* ☎ *202/687-0100. www.georgetown.edu.*

7 ★★ Cady's Alley. Looking for that perfect armchair to go with your new lamp? You'll likely find it here in D.C.'s design district. Tucked next to the C&O Canal in Georgetown, this cluster of shops features international and local contemporary furnishings, clothing, and accessories. Baker Furniture, Contemporaria, and Design within Reach are just a few of the purveyors you'll find in this lofty design center. ⏱ *1 hr. 3314 M St. NW (between 33rd and 34th sts.). www.cadysalley.com. Store hours vary.*

8 Leopold's Kafe Konditorei. Stroll through Cady's Alley behind M Street and you'll find this eclectic

eatery on the corner of the central courtyard. It's equal parts coffeehouse, restaurant, bar, and bakery, and visitors will find everything from oxtail soup to cured meats, along with traditional treats and sweets. *3315 Cady's Alley NW. 202/965-6005. www.kafeleopolds.com. $.*

⑨ C&O Canal. Perfect for families, this 184.5-mile (298km) waterway would take you to Cumberland, Maryland, if you were to follow its course. Georgetown once functioned as a large tobacco port until the mid-1800s, so workers used the canal to transport goods and materials up the Potomac River. Amble along the towpath to see quaint historic homes and original canal locks. ⏱ *2 hr. Visitor Center: 1057 Thomas Jefferson St. NW.* ☎ *202/653-5190. www.nps.gov/choh.*

⑩ ★ Old Stone House. On M Street—between modern attractions like Sephora and Hu's Shoes—is the Old Stone House, one of the capital's oldest buildings, built in 1765. Give your credit card a rest; explore its interior, and

First floor kitchen in The Old Stone House.

learn how Washingtonians lived nearly 250 years ago. ⏱ *30 min. 3051 M St. NW.* ☎ *202/895-6070. www.nps.gov/olst. Free admission. Daily 11am–6pm. Closed holidays.*

⑪ Bourbon Steak. The chic and contemporary restaurant caters to sleek Georgetowners and a who's who of Washington who enjoy a good steak—and don't mind paying $40 to $50 for one. The elegant lounge offers views of Georgetown's C&O Canal. *2800 Pennsylvania Ave. NW.* ☎ *202/944-2026. www.bourbonsteakdc.com. $$$.*

Traveling to Georgetown

Georgetown is not exactly convenient to reach. There are no Metro stops here—or even close to here; you will need to rely on bus or taxi transport for access. If you don't mind a walk, however, get off the Metro at either Foggy Bottom in D.C. or at Rosslyn, the first stop in northern Virginia (both are on the blue and orange lines), and hike 15 to 20 minutes. Foggy Bottom is a simple stroll west on Pennsylvania, which merges into M Street, Georgetown's main drag. Rosslyn is just across Key Bridge; traverse it and you're at the other end of Georgetown—perfect for a stop at Dean & Deluca for a snack. For bus schedules, check out **www.wmata.com or www.dccirculator.com**.

Penn Quarter

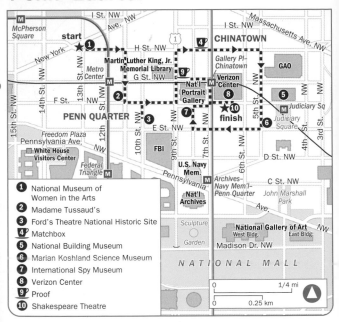

1 National Museum of Women in the Arts
2 Madame Tussaud's
3 Ford's Theatre National Historic Site
4 Matchbox
5 National Building Museum
6 Marian Koshland Science Museum
7 International Spy Museum
8 Verizon Center
9 Proof
10 Shakespeare Theatre

Just 15 years ago, this section of town induced more fear than fanfare. Now Penn Quarter has certifiably transformed, drawing beautiful young things in droves to explore it. The former red-light district has been replaced with scene-making lounges and high-end hotels. Art galleries, edgy theater companies, and groovy retailers have taken over aging buildings and given them new life. Throw in the Verizon Center for major sporting events and stadium concerts, and you've got one happening neighborhood. START: **Metro to Metro Center.**

1 National Museum of Women in the Arts. One of the lesser-known museums in the city, but nonetheless important, the NMWA is the only one dedicated solely to showcasing women artists in the country. More than 4,000 works comprise the collection of art from women from the 16th century to the present. ⏱ 1 hr. 1250 New York Ave. NW. ☎ 202/783-5000. www.nmwa. org. Metro: Metro Center.

2 ★ Madame Tussauds. Meet Presidents George Washington, Thomas Jefferson and even Barack Obama and First Lady Michelle—or at least their wax figures—at this institution that also features other important political, sports, and music figures of Washington. ⏱ 1 hr. 1001 F St. NW. www.madame tussauds.com/washington. Mon–Sat 10am–6pm; Sun 10am–4pm. Metro: Gallery Place/Chinatown.

Art installation in front of the National Museum of Women in the Arts.

❸ ★★ Ford's Theatre National Historic Site.

On April 14, 1865, gun-wielding assassin John Wilkes Booth killed President Abraham Lincoln here, as the president watched a performance of *Our American Cousin.* Booth crept into the president's box, shot Lincoln, leapt to the stage shouting "Sic semper tyrannis!" ("Thus ever to tyrants!"), and then mounted his horse in the alley and galloped off. Doctors carried Lincoln across the street to the house of William Petersen, where the president died the next morning. The theater closed immediately, and the War Department used the building as an office until 1893, when three floors collapsed, killing 22 clerks. Subsequently, the structure fell into disuse until 1968, when it reopened—restored to its appearance on the night of Lincoln's murder—as a functioning playhouse and a repository for historical artifacts surrounding the assassination and the trial of Booth's conspirators. The collection of museum artifacts includes Booth's derringer pistol, Lincoln's overcoat from the night he was shot, and the theatre binoculars that were found on the floor of the president's box.

Another recent renovation expanded exhibits, added a new lobby and box office, and installed 21st-century lighting, seats, and concessions. ⏱ *1½ hr., or more if you plan to see a show. 511 10th St. NW.* ☎ *202/347-4833. www.fords theatre.org. Museum admission $5. Performance ticket prices vary. Hours vary. Metro: Archive/Navy Memorial.*

4 Matchbox.

Built into a 15-foot (4.5m) wide, three-story tall building, this is, quite simply the place for pizza. You'll happily nosh on fire-cooked pizza pies, mini burgers, and salads. *713 H St. NW.* ☎ *202/289-4441. www.matchboxdc.com. $$.*

The gun used to kill Lincoln on display in the Ford Museum.

⑤ ★★ National Building Museum. Architects of the world, rejoice! Finally, a museum dedicated to American achievements in the building arts. The permanent collection includes thousands of photographs, architectural drawings, some 1,500 bricks, and exhibits on interior design. The "Play Work Build" exhibit displays the museum's large architectural toy collection (think Lincoln Logs and Erector Sets), with plenty of hands-on play opportunities for kids. The "House and Home" exhibit explores how everything from household goods to the process of buying a home in America has changed over the centuries. ⏱ 45 min. See p 44.

⑥ Marian Koshland Science Museum. You don't have to be a science geek to immerse yourself for hours in this small but fascinating museum. High-tech, interactive exhibits aim to provoke critical thinking about science and how it can be applied to looming issues from climate change to healthy aging to understanding how the brain works. ⏱ 2 hr. 525 E St. NW.

☎ 202/334-1201. www.koshland-science-museum.org. Admission $5 adults, $3 children 5–18. Wed–Mon 10am–6pm (last admission 5pm), except Thanksgiving, Dec 25, and Jan 1–13. Metro: Gallery Place/Chinatown.

⑦ ★★ International Spy Museum. The word "spy" used to conjure up romantic images of James Bond and trench-coated secret agents. Now, in the wake of 9/11 and terrorist cells, it's a whole new world. To study the history of espionage and the uncharted territory we now must learn to navigate, tour this museum, which features the largest collection of international espionage artifacts ever put on public display. Exhibits include a re-creation of a tunnel beneath the divided city of Berlin during the Cold War; the intelligence-gathering stories of those behind enemy lines and of those involved in planning D-Day in World War II; an exhibit on escape and evasion techniques in wartime; the tales of more recent spies, told by the CIA and FBI agents involved in identifying them; and a mockup of an intelligence agency's 21st-century

The National Building Museum.

Interactive exhibit on global warming at the Marian Koshland Science Museum.

operations center. The Spy Museum's executive director was with the CIA for 36 years and his advisory board includes two former CIA directors, two former CIA disguise chiefs, and a retired KGB general. ○ *2 hr. 800 F St. NW.* ☎ *202/393-7798. www.spymuseum.org. Metro: Gallery Place/Chinatown.*

⑧ Verizon Center. Time it right and you could catch a game of hoops by the Wizards, or the puck ish Alex Ovechkin making goals for the Caps. You might even see Taylor Swift or another touring legend in concert when you come here for stadium-size entertainment. ○ *30 min., or more if you plan to catch a game or a show. 601 F St. NW.* ☎ *202/628-3200. www.verizon center.com. Call for admission prices. Metro: Gallery Place/Chinatown.*

⑨ ★★★ Proof continues to be at the top of the heap of D.C.'s many wine bars. A tax attorney–turned-restaurateur, Mark Kuller opened this wine-centric restaurant and devoted much of his own wine collection to its list, which boasts 1,000 different bottles. A dinner of grilled swordfish or roast Pekin duck isn't bad either. *775 G St. NW.* ☎ *202/737-7663. www.proofdc. com. $$–$$$.*

⑩ ★★ Shakespeare Theatre. From *Love's Labor Lost* to *Pericles*, this renowned outfit stages the best of the Bard in one of the District's hottest new neighborhoods. Fill up on highbrow culture, then hit the town for some low-down gallivanting after the show. ○ *30 min., or more if you plan to see a show. Metro: Gallery Place/Chinatown.*

Capitol Hill

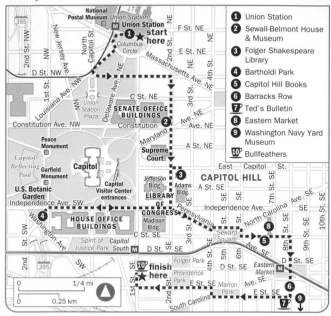

1. Union Station
2. Sewall-Belmont House & Museum
3. Folger Shakespeare Library
4. Bartholdi Park
5. Capitol Hill Books
6. Barracks Row
7. Ted's Bulletin
8. Eastern Market
9. Washington Navy Yard Museum
10. Bullfeathers

Although it's the seat of U.S. government, crowned by the Capitol's graceful dome, and encompassing the Supreme Court and the Library of Congress, "the Hill" is also a quiet residential district bounded by the Capitol in the West, the Armory to the East, H Street to the North, and the Southwest Freeway to the South. With its tree-lined streets of Victorian homes, restaurants, the U.S. Botanic Garden, and the Folger Shakespeare Library, Capitol Hill offers plenty of reasons to visit beyond its government buildings. For a more extensive tour of this historical neighborhood and its essential landmarks, see "The Best of D.C. in 2 Days" on p 14. Here are a few additional highlights, for a more relaxed day of exploration rather than sightseeing. START: **Metro to Eastern Market.**

1 Union Station. Take one step inside and you'll know that this is no typical train station. As ornate as it is functional, this 1907 Beaux Arts–style building was designed by noted architect Daniel Burnham. As a member of the illustrious

McMillan Commission (assembled in 1900 to beautify the city in a manner befitting an important world capital), Burnham counseled, "Make no little plans. They have no magic to stir men's blood." Union Station, one of the commission's

Sewall-Belmont House.

"big plans" (at its opening, it was the largest train station in the world), was modeled after the Baths of Diocletian and the Arch of Constantine in Rome. The Main Hall features a nine-story, 96-foot (29m) barrel-vaulted ceiling inlaid with 70 pounds (32 kilograms) of 22-carat gold-leaf, acres of white marble floors punctuated by red Champlain dots, bronze grilles, and rich Honduran mahogany paneling. The adjacent East Hall has scagliola marble walls and columns; a gorgeous, hand-stenciled skylight ceiling; and stunning murals inspired by the frescoes of Pompeii. In the heyday of rail travel, many

Union Station.

important events took place in Union Station: Visiting royalty and heads of state were honored here, as were World War I General Pershing, upon his return from France; South Pole explorer Rear Admiral Byrd; and President Franklin Delano Roosevelt, whose funeral train was met here by thousands of mourners in 1945. Today Union Station is a crossroads for D.C. locals, commuters from Baltimore and the suburbs, and visitors from farther afield. It also houses loads of shops such as Nine West, Swatch, and Victoria's Secret, plus a solid section of fast food and fine-fare dining options. ◷ *30 min. 2 Massachusetts Ave. NE.* ☎ *202/371-9441. www.unionstationdc.com. Free admission. Daily 24 hr. Metro: Union Station.*

❷ **Sewall-Belmont House & Museum.** You might find yourself humming "Sister Suffragette" from *Mary Poppins*—"We're clearly soldiers in petticoats, and dauntless crusaders for women's votes"—as you tour this museum. This Federal/Queen Anne–style house was once the home of Alice Paul (1885–1977), who founded the National Women's Party in 1913 and wrote the original Equal Rights Amendment to the Constitution (ERA). Paul, who held three law degrees and a Ph.D.

Brenda Putnam's statue of Puck stands in the garden of the Folger Shakespeare Library.

in sociology, was jailed seven times in the U.S. and Great Britain for the cause of women's suffrage. Paul lived here from 1929 to 1972, but now the National Women's Party owns and maintains the house. Exhibitions trace the path of the women's movement, from the better-known activist Susan B. Anthony, to 59¢ buttons and the ERA. Check out picketing banners, 5,000 prints and photographs, original cartoons, more than 50 scrapbooks from early suffragists, paintings, sculptures, publications, and more. ① *1 hr. 144 Constitution Ave. NE. ☎ 202/ 546-1210. www.sewallbelmont.org. Admission $8. Open for tours on Fri and Sat at 11am, 1, and 3pm. Metro: Union Station.*

❸ ★★ **Folger Shakespeare Library.** Founded in 1932 by ardent Shakespeare fan (and wealthy Standard Oil executive) Henry Clay Folger and his wife, Emily, this repository houses the world's largest collection of the Bard's printed works. In addition to its 160,000 books—many of which are classified as rare—the library also provides an important research center for students of the master playwright and Renaissance literature. The permanent exhibits in the Great Hall include period costumes, musical instruments, historic playbills, and more. ① *45 min. 201 E. Capitol St. SE. ☎ 202/544-7077. www.folger.edu. Mon–Sat 10am– 5pm; Sun noon–5pm; with docent tours Mon–Sat at 11am, 1, and 3pm and Sun at noon and 3pm; closed on federal holidays. Metro: Capitol South or Union Station.*

❹ ★★ **Bartholdi Park.** Part of the U.S. Botanic Garden, this flower-filled park is about the size of a city block and is named for the French sculptor who created its 30-foot-high (9m) cast-iron "fountain of light and water." Frederic Auguste Bartholdi (1834–1904), who is most famous for that other large sculpture he did—the Statue of Liberty in New York Harbor—constructed this work for the 1876 International Exposition in Philadelphia. When the exposition closed, the U.S. government purchased the sculpture for the National Mall; it was moved to its current location in 1932. Come to view it, and to enjoy the surrounding sunflowers, petunias, morning glories, tall ornamental grasses, and creeping vines. ① *45 min. 1st St. and Independence Ave. SW. Free admission. Daily 10am–5pm. Metro: Union Station.*

5 Capitol Hill Books. This spot is a mecca for bibliophiles and lovers of used books. Spend some time wandering this quirky book maze and you'll find some of the more unique titles in literary history. ⏱ 30 min. 657 C St. SE. ☎ 202/544-162. www.capitolhill books-dc.com. Mon–Fri 11:30am–6pm. Sat–Sun 9am–6pm. Metro: Eastern Market.

6 ★★ Barracks Row. The strip along 8th St., SE, became the first commercial center in D.C. after Thomas Jefferson centered the Marine Corps there in 1801. The neighborhood has ridden out some downturns since then, but in more recent years, Washingtonians have flocked to the lively district for housing, dining, and shopping. Restaurants, outdoor cafes, and taverns such as the Ugly Mug and Belga Café are always packed, and stores such as Metro Mutts and Homebody cater to those seeking one-of-a-kind finds. ⏱ 1 hr. 8th and I sts. SE. ☎ 202/544-3188. www. barracksrow.org. Metro: Eastern Market.

7 ★ Ted's Bulletin. Capitol Hill is known for its stuffy, only-in-D.C. restaurants, but this lively American eatery, with close tables and a neighborly feel, is anything but. Dig

The Bartholdi Park Fountain is dramatically lit at night.

into delicious salads and burgers, but save room for dessert—the milkshakes and pies are top-notch here. 505 8th St. SE. 202/544-8337. www.tedsbulletin.com. $–$$.

8 ★★ Eastern Market. You'll have many "have-to-have-it" moments during your stroll through the shops of this D.C. landmark that has been in continuous operation since 1873. A 2007 fire nearly decimated the 135-year-old East Hall building, but the city government—and devoted fans of the market—vowed to rebuild it and it reopened in 2009. Snack on treats

Bustling Eastern Market.

from various vendors to stay fueled as you browse the wares of more than 175 exhibitors who showcase their handmade pottery, jewelry, crafts, furniture, and—on the weekends—fresh produce from the surrounding states. Saturday morning is the best time to go experience a D.C. tradition: blueberry pancakes at the Market Lunch counter. ⏱ *2 hr. 7th St. & North Carolina Ave., SE.* ☎ *202/543-7293 or 703/534-7612. Tues–Fri 7am–7pm, Sat 7am–6pm, Sun 9am–5pm. Metro: Eastern Market.*

❾ Washington Navy Yard Museum. If you're already in the Capitol Hill area, it's a relatively short walk to the Washington Navy Yard and Museum. Off the beaten track and often overlooked—and thus, blessedly uncrowded—this museum celebrates the Navy's heroes, ships, diplomacy, and battles. Among its many exhibits are submarines, swords, and firearms from Revolutionary ship captains, artifacts from salvaged Naval vessels dating back to 1800, and a range of Naval uniforms that span the years. ⏱ *1 hr. 805 Kidder Breese SE.* ☎ *202/433-4882. www.history.navy.gov. Mon–Fri 9am–5pm, Sat–Sun 10am–5pm. Call in advance for access information, unless traveling with active or retired military*

A gun at the Navy Yard Museum.

escort. Free admission. Metro: Eastern Market or Navy Yard.

❿ Bullfeathers. Everyone—Democrats, Republicans, staffers, and Hill members—head to this venerable institution for strong drinks when the working day is done. Eavesdrop on conversations and you might just hear some of those famous D.C. secrets. *410 1st St. SE.* ☎ *202/484-0228. www.bullfeathersdc.net. $$.* ●

Shopping Best Bets

Best **Interior Design District**
★★ Cady's Alley, 3314 M St. NW,
Georgetown (p 110)

Best **Antiques (to \$10K)**
Carling Nichols, 1655 Wisconsin
Ave. NW (see "Antique Row," p 110)

Best **Antiques (to \$100)**
★★ Eastern Market, 7th St. and
North Carolina Ave. SE (p 112)

Best **"Bling"**
★★★ Tiny Jewel Box, 1155 Connecticut Ave., NW (p 111)

Best **Shoes for \$500**
★★ Hu's Shoes, 3005 M St. NW.
(p 112)

Best **Shoes for \$50**
Nine West, 1029 Connecticut Ave.
NW (p 108)

Best **Apparel for Serious
Fashionistas**
★★ Cusp, 3030 M St. NW (p 107)

Best **Commercial Shopping
Drag**
M Street and Wisconsin Avenue

Best **Hidden Gem**
Home Rule, 1807 14th St. NW
(p 110)

Best **Hood for Contemporary
Art**
The Galleries on 14th Street, 14th
St. NW (p 106)

Best **Place for a Power Tie**
★★★ Thomas Pink, 1127 Connecticut Ave. NW (p 108)

Best for **Gourmet Snacks**
★ Dean & Deluca, 3276 M St. NW
(p 108)

Best **Flowers**
★ Ultra Violet Flowers, 1218 31st
St. NW (p 109)

Best Bookstore to **Catch a Senator Reading about Himself**
★ Capitol Hill Books, 657 C St. SE
(p 106)

Best for Cool **Mid-20th-
Century Finds**
Miss Pixie's, 1626 14th St. NW
(p 110)

Best **Baby Stuff**
★★ Dawn Price Baby, 3112 M St.
NW (p 106)

Best **Contemporary Home
Design**
Room & Board, 1840 14th St. NW
(p 110)

Best **Cards & Gifts**
★ The Dandelion Patch, 1663 Wisconsin Ave. NW (p 109)

Best for **Musicians**
Middle C Music, 4530 Wisconsin
Ave. NW (p 111)

Best **Bones to Pick**
★★ Metro Mutts, 508 H St. NE
(p 111)

Best **for Innovative Children's
Toys**
★ Tugooh Toys, 1355 Wisconsin
Ave. NW (p 106)

Previous page: Shop for up and coming
designer names at Cusp.

Capitol Hill & Penn Quarter

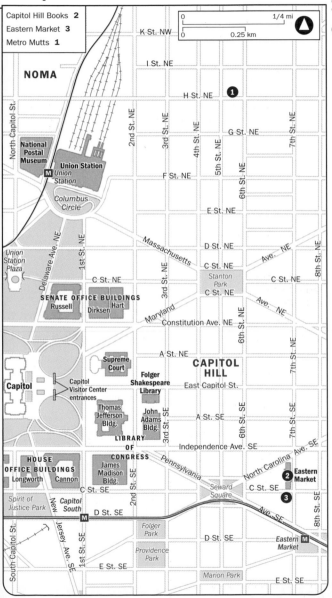

Capitol Hill Books **2**
Eastern Market **3**
Metro Mutts **1**

K St. NW

I St. NE

NOMA

H St. NE **1**

North Capitol St.

2nd St. NE
3rd St. NE
4th St. NE
5th St. NE
6th
7th St. NE

G St. NE

National Postal Museum

Union Station
Ⓜ Union Station

F St. NE

Columbus Circle

E St. NE

Delaware Ave. NE
1st St. NE

Massachusetts

D St. NE

Ave. NE
8th St. NE

Union Station Plaza

C St. NE

3rd St. NE

C St. NE

Stanton Park

C St. NE

SENATE OFFICE BUILDINGS
Russell   Dirksen   Hart

Maryland

Ave. NE

6th St. NE

Constitution Ave. NE

A St. NE

7th St. NE

Capitol

Supreme Court

CAPITOL HILL

Capitol Visitor Center entrances

Folger Shakespeare Library

East Capitol St.

Thomas Jefferson Bldg.

John Adams Bldg.

3rd St. SE

A St. SE

5th St. SE

6th St. SE

7th St. SE

LIBRARY OF CONGRESS

Independence Ave. SE

HOUSE OFFICE BUILDINGS
Longworth   Cannon

James Madison Bldg.

Pennsylvania

North Carolina Ave. SE

2 **Eastern Market**

C St. SE

2nd St. SE

Seward Square

C St. SE

3

Spirit of Justice Park

Capitol South

New

D St. SE

Ⓜ

Ave. SE

8th St. SE

South Capitol St.

Jersey Ave. SE

1st St. SE

Folger Park

D St. SE

Eastern Market Ⓜ

E St. SE

Providence Park

Marion Park

E St. SE

0   1/4 mi
0   0.25 km

Georgetown & Dupont Circle

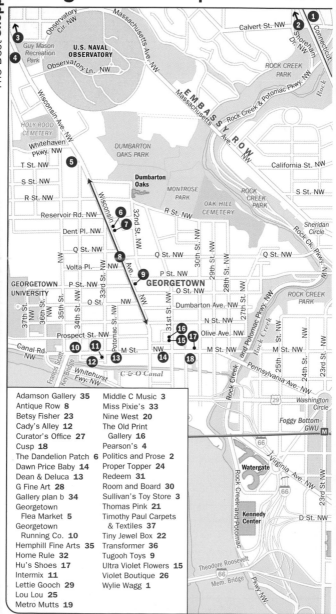

Adamson Gallery **35**
Antique Row **8**
Betsy Fisher **23**
Cady's Alley **12**
Curator's Office **27**
Cusp **18**
The Dandelion Patch **6**
Dawn Price Baby **14**
Dean & Deluca **13**
G Fine Art **28**
Gallery plan b **34**
Georgetown
    Flea Market **5**
Georgetown
    Running Co. **10**
Hemphill Fine Arts **35**
Home Rule **32**
Hu's Shoes **17**
Intermix **11**
Lettie Gooch **29**
Lou Lou **25**
Metro Mutts **19**

Middle C Music **3**
Miss Pixie's **33**
Nine West **20**
The Old Print
    Gallery **16**
Pearson's **4**
Politics and Prose **2**
Proper Topper **24**
Redeem **31**
Room and Board **30**
Sullivan's Toy Store **3**
Thomas Pink **21**
Timothy Paul Carpets
    & Textiles **37**
Tiny Jewel Box **22**
Transformer **36**
Tugooh Toys **9**
Ultra Violet Flowers **15**
Violet Boutique **26**
Wylie Wagg **1**

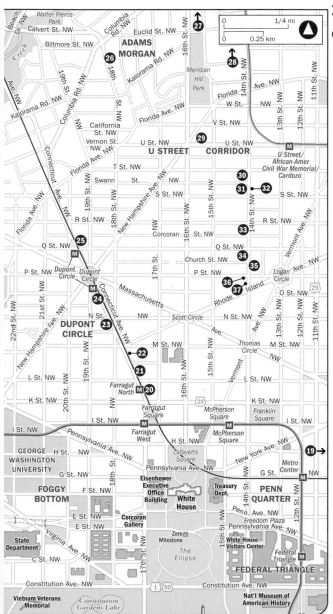

Shopping A to Z

Art

★★★ The Galleries on 14th Street

14TH STREET/LOGAN CIRCLE   This main street is known for its intimate galleries featuring modern and contemporary works. Don't miss these highlights: **G Fine Art** (4758 14th St. NW; ☎ 202/462-1601; www.gfineartdc.com; no credit cards); **Hemphill Fine Arts** (1515 14th St. NW #300 ☎ 202/234-5601; www.hemphillfinearts.com; AE, DC, DISC, MC, V); **Adamson Gallery** (1515 14th St. NW ☎ 202/232-0707; www.adamsongallery.com; MC, V); **Curator's Office** (1469 Harvard St. REAR NW ☎ 202/360-2573; www.curatorsoffice.com; MC, V); **Transformer** (1404 P St. NW, at 14th St.; ☎ 202/483-1102; www.transformerdc.org); and **Gallery plan b** (1530 14th St., NW, at Q St.; ☎ 202/234-2711; www.galleryplanb.com; AE, MC, V). Metro: Cardozo/U St. Map p 104.

Babies & Kids

★★ Dawn Price Baby

GEORGETOWN   If you're a member of the stroller set whose bundle of joy must have the latest Bugaboo model, head to this small but stocked shop. Clothing, shoes, and toys are also for sale. 3112 M St. NW (at 31st St.). ☎ 202/333-3939. www.dawnpricebaby.com. AE, DC, DISC, MC, V. No Metro access. See "Traveling to Georgetown" on p 91. Map p 104.

★ Sullivan's Toy Store

CLEVELAND PARK   Forgot to pack Elmo? This tantrum-quashing shop is jam-packed with every conceivable plaything, puzzle, costume, wheeled wonder, art supply, and entertaining distraction imaginable. 4200 Wisconsin Ave. (at Newark St.). ☎ 202/362-1343. AE, DISC, MC, V. Metro: Cleveland Park, then walk west to Wisconsin. Map p 104.

★ Tugooh Toys

GEORGETOWN   If you're picky about toys, then head to this thoughtful shop, which is well stocked with an array of all-natural and eco-friendly toys, games, books, and clothes. 1355 Wisconsin Ave. NW. ☎ 202/333-9476. www.tugoohtoys.com AE, DISC, MC, V. No Metro Access. See "Traveling to Georgetown," on p 91. Map p 104.

Books

★ Capitol Hill Books

CAPITOL HILL   Feel like losing yourself on a rainy afternoon in dusty stacks bursting with amazing old books? Steps from Eastern Market, this used books store has more than a century's worth of history and is a goldmine for modern first editions, lit-crit, and unusual subjects. 657 C St. SE (between 6th and 7th sts.). ☎ 202/544-1621. www.capitolhillbooks-dc.com. AE, DC, MC, V. Metro: Eastern Market. Map p 103.

★★ Politics and Prose

CLEVELAND PARK   If on principle you'd rather give your hard-earned cash to Mom and Pop than a big chain, head north of downtown to this two-story shop. It's famed in D.C. for its warm vibe, nearly nightly author readings, excellent selection, and cozy coffeehouse. 5015 Connecticut Ave. NW (at Fessenden St.). ☎ 202/364-1919. www.politics-prose.com. AE, DISC, MC, V. Metro: Van Ness–UDC, then walk or transfer to an "L" bus for 1 mile (1.6km). Map p 104.

Fashion

★ Betsy Fisher

DUPONT CIRCLE   You follow Vogue, so peruse the racks of this boutique—buzz to

Enjoy author readings at Politics and Prose bookstore in Cleveland Park.

gain entry, please—designed to suit the caviar tastes of well-dressed women who must look smashing at D.C. dinner parties and occasional dates with high-ranking officials. *1224 Connecticut Ave. NW (at 18th St.). ☎ 202/785-1975. www.betsyfisher.com. AE, DISC, MC, V. Metro: Dupont Circle. Map p 104.*

★★ **Cusp** GEORGETOWN   Sister to the Neiman Marcus chain, this one-off boutique carries the latest designer duds, plus the best up-and-coming names. Shoes, handbags and other accessories are also found here. *3030 M St. NW. ☎ 202/625-0893. www.cusp.com. AE, DISC, MC, V. No Metro access. See "Traveling to Georgetown," on p 91. Map p 104.*

Georgetown Running Co.
GEORGETOWN   If you're light on your feet—meaning the prospect of running 5 miles (8km) fills you with joy, not dread—jog this way for state-of-the-art shoes and gear. *3401 M St. NW (at 34th St.). ☎ 202/337-8626. AE, DISC, MC, V. No Metro access. See "Traveling to Georgetown" on p 91. Map p 104.*

★★ **Intermix** GEORGETOWN   What started in NYC has landed in D.C.: a satellite store for Marc Jacobs jackets, Diane von Furstenberg wrap dresses, rhinestone cowboy boots, Norma Kamali jumpsuits, and oversize shades—priced to make you feel as though the paparazzi are waiting at the front door. *3300 M St. NW (at Wisconsin Ave.). ☎ 202/298-8080. www.intermixonline.com. AE, DC, DISC, MC, V. No Metro access. See "Traveling to Georgetown" on p 91. Map p 104.*

Fashionable D.C. women head to Betsy Fisher's boutique for classy designer pieces.

Proper Topper carries funky clothes and gifts in addition to all sorts of hats.

Lettie Gooch SHAW You'll find an NYC Soho vibe in this unique boutique that stocks one-of-a-kind feminine fashions from Tricia Fix, SaltWorks, Hype, Jak & Rae, and local designers. *1921 8th St. NW. Suite 110* ☎ *202/332-4242. www. lettiegooch.com. Metro: U Street/ Cardozo. Map p 104.*

Lou Lou DUPONT CIRCLE Head to this boutique for a bonanza of accessories, from beaded necklaces to brooches to headbands and handbags—all at very reasonable prices. Then visit its adjacent clothing store for fun apparel. *1601 Connecticut Ave. NW. Nearby locations on L Street, Georgetown, Penn Quarter and Bethesda.* ☎ *202/588-0027. www.loulouboutiques.com. AE, MC, V. Metro: Dupont Circle. Map p 104.*

Nine West DOWNTOWN *Already well-known from coast to coast, this stand-alone outpost carries inexpensive boots, espadrilles, and flats to have you stepping pretty in the city. 1029 Connecticut Ave. NW.* ☎ *202/331-3243. www.ninewest. com. Metro: Farragut North. Map p 104.*

Proper Topper DUPONT CIRCLE From the name alone, you can probably guess what this tiny shop specializes in. Every type of hat, cap, and beret in stylish designs, along with picture frames, gift books, and funky clothes. *1350 Connecticut Ave. NW.* ☎ *202/842-3055. www.propertopper.com. Metro: Dupont Circle. Map p 104.*

Redeem 14TH STREET Male fashions are so often left out of the boutique apparel scene in D.C. Not so at this store, which features designer wear and edgy apparel for both men and women. *1810 14th St. NW.* ☎ *202/332-7447. www. redeemus.com. Metro: U Street/Cardozo. Map p 104.*

★★★ Thomas Pink DOWNTOWN Dapper gentlemen from the nation's capital descend upon this outpost of the London-based brand for well-cut business suits, power ties, cufflinks, crisp and colorful shirts, and tailored service. Inside the Mayflower Hotel. *1127 Connecticut Ave. NW (between L and M sts.).* ☎ *202/223-5390. www. thomaspink.com. AE, MC, V. Metro: Farragut North. Map p 104.*

Expert staff can help guide your wine or liquor selection at Pearson's.

Friendship Heights, D.C.

Known and loved for its boutiques and shops, this bustling strip is billed as D.C.'s Fifth Avenue. If it's the extremely high-end you're looking for, take a 15-minute Metro ride—or better yet, hail a cab—to this busy Wisconsin Avenue corridor that caters to luxury buyers with outposts of Sak's Fifth Avenue, Tiffany's, Louis Vuitton, Jimmy Choo, Neiman Marcus, Bloomingdales, and more. Be prepared to drop some serious Benjamins on designer dresses, impeccable suits, handbags, and jewelry in this pricey neighborhood along the Maryland border. *Wisconsin and Western aves. Metro: Friendship Heights.*

★ **Violet Boutique.** ADAMS MORGAN   Chat with savvy owner Julie Egermayer or one of her associates, and you'll quickly see why this store is best for finding fun, trendy looks and accessories—all priced under $100. *2439 18th St. NW.* ☎ *202/621-9225. www.violetdc.com. Metro: Woodley Park-Zoo/Adams Morgan. Map p 104.*

Flowers & Gifts
★ **The Dandelion Patch.** GEORGETOWN   This picture-perfect shop offers invitations & announcements for all occasions, plus beautiful stationery and cards. *1663 Wisconsin Ave. NW.* ☎ *202/333-8803. www.thedandelionpatch.com. MC, V. No Metro access. See "Traveling to Georgetown" on p 91. Map p 104.*

★ **Ultra Violet Flowers** GEORGETOWN   In the doghouse? Wooing your beloved? Mother's Day? No matter. Call Ultra Violet for a floral concoction exploding with color and sweet, intoxicating scents. *1218 31st St. NW (near M St.).* ☎ *202/333-3002. www.ultravioletflowersdc.com. AE, MC, V. No Metro access. See "Traveling to Georgetown" on p 91. Map p 104.*

Food & Wine
★ **Dean & Deluca** GEORGETOWN   Crave a dark chocolate bar from Switzerland? How about a custard fruit tart? Gourmands with a nose for fragrant cheeses, fresh fish, out-of-season fruit, choice-cut meats, aged wines, Kona coffee beans, and European crackers nosh and shop here. In fine weather, try lunch at the outdoor cafe. *3276 M St. NW (at Potomac St.).* ☎ *202/342-2500. www.deandeluca.com. AE, DISC, MC, V. No Metro access. See "Traveling to Georgetown" on p 91. Map p 104.*

★ **Pearson's** GLOVER PARK   This neighborhood standby sells more than 2,000 fine wines, liquours, and spirits. A knowledgeable staff of 15 experts hosts regular wine tastings. *2436 Wisconsin Ave. NW (37th St.).* ☎ *202/333-6666. www.pearsonswine.com. MC, V. Bus line: D1 or D2. Map p 104.*

Furniture & Home Design
Antique Row GEORGETOWN   Depending on which way you're walking, Antique Row is either a cool cruise downhill or a steep trek up it. In any event, antiques lovers won't care—they'll be too busy gaping at the

Shop for funky housewares and bath items at Home Rule.

storefronts with mint-condition, 18th-century divans; beautifully painted Persian consoles; weathered ceramic water jugs; and other singular finds. The best of the lot: Carling Nichols (see below); Jean Pierre Antiques and, for early-20th-century fans, Random Harvest. Bring your Black AmEx card for this shopping stroll—prices are that steep. *Wisconsin Ave., from S St. to N St. No Metro access. See "Traveling to Georgetown" on p 91. Map p 104.*

★★ **Cady's Alley** GEORGETOWN Make tracks to Washington's district devoted to furnishings and accessories. Not long ago, Cady's Alley was all industrial space and abandoned lofts. Now, if you walk through a bricked archway off M Street and descend a flight of stairs into a hidden alcove, you'll discover shops such as Contemporaria for Italian furniture, Bulthaup for ultraluxe culinary gadgets, Circa Lighting for European lighting, and Poggenpohl Studio for German kitchen fixtures. *3300 block of M St. NW. www.cadysalley.com. No Metro access. See "Traveling to Georgetown" on p 91. Map p 104.*

Carling Nichols. GEORGETOWN Peruse a wide selection of 17th-, 18th-, and 19th-century antiques and fine art, and be prepared to spend, at this antiques company in Georgetown. *1655 Wisconsin Ave. NW. ☎ 202/338-5600. www.carling nichols.com. No Metro access. See "Traveling to Georgetown," on p 91.*

Home Rule U STREET Funky furnishings, housewares, kitchen gadgets, and bath items are packed into this storefront. Have a kid who likes to cook? You'll find great gifts of all varieties here. *1807 14th St. NW. ☎ 202/797-5544. www.home rule.com. Metro: U Street/Cardozo. Map p 104.*

Miss Pixie's U STREET Scavenger hunters will love Miss Pixie's giant new space that's filled with secondhand furnishings, funky

Cady's Alley district is the place to shop for light fixtures, kitchen gadgets, and other home furnishings.

Timothy Paul Carpets and Textiles.

chandeliers, table settings, figurines, and other crazy knick-knacks (plastic flamingos, anyone?). *1626 14th St. NW.* ☎ *202/232-8171. www.misspixies.com. Metro: U Street/Cardozo. Map p 104.*

Room & Board 14TH STREET
Do you groove on sleek sofas, stainless steel coffee tables, or mid-20th-century chairs? Room & Board, housed in a restored 1919 Ford Motors showroom, is a must for simple, modern furniture. *1840 14th St. NW.* ☎ *202/ 729-8300. www.roomandboard.com. Metro: U Street/Cardozo. Map p 104.*

The Old Print Gallery.
GEORGETOWN Fans of old prints and maps from the 16th century and later will revel in this tiny shop's collection that features only originals—no reproductions—many with scenes of D.C. *1220 31st St. NW.* ☎ *202/683-3950. www.old printgallery.com. No Metro access.* See "Traveling to Georgetown," on p 91. Map p 104.

Timothy Paul Carpets & Textiles LOGAN CIRCLE Interior design enthusiasts should make a beeline to this husband-and-wife-owned boutique/gallery specializing in custom-colored textiles, upscale carpet lines, antique rugs, and unusual lighting fixtures. *1429B 14th St. NW (btw P and Q Sts.).* ☎ *202/ 234-2020. www.timothypaulcarpets. com. AE, MC, V. Metro: McPherson Square or Dupont Circle. Map p 104.*

Jewelry
★★★ **Tiny Jewel Box.** DOWNTOWN Thinking of popping the question or surprising your sweetie with a fabulous bauble, expensive watch, or eye-popping ring from an estate sale? Look no further than this D.C. mainstay, a peddler of romantic, unique adornments. *1155 Connecticut Ave. NW.* ☎ *202/393-2747. www. tinyjewelbox.com. AE, MC, V. Metro: Farragut North. Map p 104.*

Music
Middle C Music. TENLEYTOWN Looking for the perfect drum set or sheet music for the aspiring musician? Stop in to this packed shop that carries music of all genres, accessories, gifts, and books—and hosts lessons. *4530 Wisconsin Ave. NW.* ☎ *202/244-7326. www.middle cmusic.com. DISC, MC, V. Metro: Tenleytown. Map p 104.*

Pets
★★ **Metro Mutts** H STREET Spoiled felines and diva dogs know where to send their masters for all-organic kibble; irresistible catnip; pigs' ears; and designer bones, collars, harnesses, and other supplies. *508 H St. NE.* ☎ *202/450-5661. www.metromuttsdc.com. AE, DISC, MC, V. Metro: Eastern Market. Map p 104.*

Wylie Wagg. WOODLEY PARK
Fido gets the star treatment here, where you can grab gourmet treats, supplies, and toys. Even birds and

Eastern Market's indoor space is open year-round.

bunnies are taken care of at this cute store. *2625 Connecticut Ave., NW.* ☎ *202/506-7007. www. wyliewagg.com. Metro: Woodley Park/Zoo. Map p 104.*

Shoes

★★ Hu's Shoes GEORGETOWN A rather daunting showroom—you might be the only customer fending off several hungry salespeople—displays the latest and greatest in women's "rebellious" designer shoes, including Sonia Rykiel, Chloé, Proenza Schouler, and more. *3005 M St. NW (at 30th St.).* ☎ *202/342-0202. www.*

Georgetown Flea Market is open every Sunday, weather permitting.

husonline.com. AE, DC, DISC, MC, V. No Metro access. See "Traveling to Georgetown" on p 91 Map p 104.

★★ Eastern Market CAPITOL HILL If Washingtonians could name only one institution endemic to the city that had nothing to do with politics, 9 out of 10 would say Eastern Market. Locals gather here on weekends for the flea market, outdoor vendors, artisans, and brunch spots. Its permanent buildings are open year-round, Tuesday through Sunday; the outdoor lot fills on weekends (Mar–Dec) with farmers and fresh produce, plus bargain-hunters looking to score great deals. *306 7th St. SE (between North Carolina Ave. and C St. SE).* ☎ *202/544-0083. www.eastern marketdc.com. Metro: Eastern Market. Map p 103.*

Georgetown Flea Market

GEORGETOWN Every Sunday (unless it's pouring rain or freezing cold outside), bargain hunters troll the lot at the Corcoran School for cheap treasures. Score handmade and antique jewelry, velvet Elvis paintings, secondhand leather jackets, and used furniture from weathered vendors smoking cigarettes, ready to haggle. *Wisconsin Ave. NW (at Whitehaven St. NW). No Metro access. See "Traveling to Georgetown" on p 91. Map p 104.* ●

Rock Creek Park

1. Rock Creek Park Planetarium
2. Rock Creek Horse Center
3. Picnic in the park
4. Rock Creek Park Tennis Center
5. Carter Barron Amphitheatre

Boundary Bridge
Parkside Dr.
Beach Dr.
Rock Creek
Kalmia Rd.
17th St.
Juniper St.
Wise Rd.
Holly St.
Holly St.
29

MARYLAND
DISTRICT OF COLUMBIA
Chestnut St.
Beech
Aberfoyle Pl.
Western Ave.
31st St.
Oregon Ave.
Tennyson St.
Rittenhouse St.
Bingham Dr.
WESTERN RIDGE TRAIL
Pinehurst Branch
Riley Spring Bridge

Alaska Ave.
WALTER REED ARMY MEDICAL CENTER
Aspen St.
Whittier St.
16th St.

Rolling Meadow Bridge
Rittenhouse St.
Battleground National Cemetery
Fort Stevens

Milkhouse Ford
Miller Cabin
Fort DeRussy
Military Joyce Rd.
Rd.
Manchester Ln.

LITTLE FOREST PARK
Nebraska Ave.
30th St.
Military Rd.
27th St.
Grant Rd.
Nature Center and Planetarium
Park Police Rock Creek Station
Kennedy St.
Rock Creek
Morrow Dr.

Broad Branch
Glover Rd.
Ross Dr.
Beach Dr.
VALLEY TRAIL
Ballfields
13th St.

Connecticut Ave.
Brandywine St.
Albemarle St.
29th St.
Broad Branch
Rapids Bridge
Parking
Box Office
Boulder Bridge
17th St.

Equitation Field
Audubon Ter.
SOAPSTONE VALLEY PARK
Van Ness-UDC
Van Ness St.
Rodman St.
Porter St.
Cleveland Park
Peirce Barn
Tilden St.
Quarry
Peirce Mill
Tennis Courts
Bluff Bridge
Porter St.
Park Headquarters Klingle Mansion
Beach Dr.
Klingle Rd.
Woodley Rd.
Klingle
Washington National Cathedral
NATIONAL ZOOLOGICAL PARK
Adams Mill Rd.

Pulpit Rock
Upshur St.
Jules Jusserand Memorial
Piney Branch Pkwy.
16th St.
Arkansas Ave.
Colorado Ave.
Blagden Ave.
29
Park Rd.

1/2 mi
0.5 km

Previous page: The Smithsonian Castle.

ow many other major American urban areas have 3,000 acres (1,214 hectares) of natural woodlands smack dab in the middle of the city? Established in 1890 by the Rock Creek Park Historic District and protected by the U.S. Congress, this green resource is to Washingtonians what Central Park is to New Yorkers—except New Yorkers can't camp, canoe, or lose themselves for miles on trails that wind beneath canopies of lush-leaved trees, so thick in spots that civilization seems a distant memory. Accessible through numerous entrance points throughout northwest Washington, this urban oasis offers shade and cooler temperatures on hot days; historic parks; great golf, horseback riding, and bird watching; a refuge for deer and raccoons; and even a 1-mile (1.6km) stretch of rapids. It also borders the National Zoo. It does have isolated areas, however, so avoid visiting early in the morning or past dusk. Remain alert, and avoid going alone if you can. START: **Metro to Friendship Heights or Fort Trotten, then the E2 bus to Glover (also called Oregon) and Military roads; walk 300 feet (30m) south on the trail to the planetarium.**

Tip

Explore Rock Creek Park's activities and offerings at www.nps.gov/rocr. The park runs along Rock Creek and its tributaries from the National Zoo to the D.C. boundary. *Accessible to the public 24 hr. Metro: Woodley Park–Zoo.*

❶ ★ kids The Rock Creek Park Planetarium and Nature Center. Stargazers come to the Planetarium to stare at the heavens. Track the night skies here with the whole family, and take your little

ones (ages 4 and up, please) to special astronomical programs on the weekends. The Nature Center is also the scene of numerous activities, including nature films, crafts demonstrations, live animal demonstrations, guided nature walks, and a daily mix of lectures and other events. Self-guided nature trails begin here. All activities are free, but for planetarium shows you need to pick up tickets a half-hour in advance. There are also nature exhibits on the premises. For a schedule, check out www.nps.gov/rocr/planyourvisit/planetarium.htm.

Bike riding through Rock Creek Park.

Rock Creek Park offers visitors 3,000 acres (1,214 hectares) of unsullied grounds to wander.

Not far from the Nature Center is **Fort DeRussey,** one of 68 fortifications erected to defend the city of Washington during the Civil War. From the intersection of Military Road and Oregon Avenue, walk a short trail through the woods to reach the fort, the remains of which include high earth mounds with openings where guns were mounted, surrounded by a deep ditch/moat. ⏱ *2 hr.*

② ★★ kids **The Rock Creek Horse Center.** Next door to the planetarium, beginners can take private lessons in the ring, and more experienced riders can sign up for trail rides on weekdays with a professional trail guide. Supervised pony rides for very young

Rock Creek Park has 30 picnic areas scattered throughout its grounds.

children are also quite popular; your tyke must be at least 30 inches (.76m) tall and at least 2½ years old to join in the fun. ⏱ *1 hr. 5100 Glover Rd.* ☎ *202/362-0117. www. rockcreekhorsecenter.com. Mon–Fri 10am–6pm; Sat–Sun 9am–5pm.*

③ **Picnic in the park.** Once you enter wooded Rock Creek Park, you won't stumble upon too many fast-food joints in the underbrush. Bring along a lunch and stop at any of the 30 picnic areas throughout the grounds; some have rain shelters. Reservations required for groups of 25 and more. *Reservations may be made online at www. recreation.gov or by phone at 877/444-6777 (10am–10pm). Reservations are by the half-day.*

④ **Rock Creek Park Tennis Center.** The home of the annual Citi Open offers excellent hard and soft court facilities, a pro shop, and a stadium (16th and Kennedy sts. NW; reservations: ☎ 202/722-5949; www.rockcreektennis.com). Free tennis courts can be found throughout the District. If you love a good match and aren't too particular about the state of the facilities— expect faded hard courts, piles of leaves in the corners, and somewhat sagging nets—hurry to public parks such as Montrose (R St., between 30th and 31st sts.), Rose (P and 28th

Theodore Roosevelt Island Park

A serene, 91-acre wilderness preserve, ★★ **Theodore Roosevelt Island Park** (☎ **703/289-2500;** www.nps.gov/this) is a memorial to the nation's 26th president and his contributions to conservation. The swamp, marsh, and upland forest comprise a haven for rabbits, chipmunks, great owls, foxes, muskrats, turtles, and groundhogs. You can observe these flora and fauna in their natural environs on 2.5 miles (4km) of foot trails. It's open daily dawn to dusk, and admission is free.

By car, take the George Washington Memorial Parkway exit north from the Theodore Roosevelt Bridge. Parking is accessible only from the northbound lane; a pedestrian bridge connects the lot to the island. Or take the Metro to Rosslyn, and then walk toward the Key Bridge. A short trail under the parkway leads to the parking lot. You can also rent a canoe at Thompson's Boat Center (☎ 202/333-9543; www.thompsonboatcenter.com) and paddle over. Allow 3 hours to explore, including the commute.

sts.), and Volta (34th and Volta sts.) in Georgetown, and wait your turn. Courtesy allows for players to use the courts for 1 hour before relinquishing them to those waiting on the sidelines. ⏱ *1 hr.*

⑤ ★★★ Carter Barron Amphitheater. Want to see Shakespeare under the stars, or catch a symphony concert or dance performance? This amphitheater, in Rock Creek Park on Colorado Avenue off 17th Street, seats several thousand patrons. It opened in 1950 to commemorate the 150th anniversary of Washington as the nation's capital city. More than 60 years later, it's a local favorite among nature lovers and theater fans.

Some shows are free but may require tickets, distributed on the day of performance at the Carter Barron Box Office (noon–8pm). For shows that require tickets, prices vary. Tickets are available at the Carter Barron Box Office, or through Ticketmaster outlets (www.

ticketmaster.com). **Note:** All sales are final, even if the show is canceled; in this unlucky case, customers forfeit their tickets. *Bus: S2 and S4. Take 16th St. N, and get off at Colorado Ave.*

Rock Creek Park's shaded pathways provide a cool respite from the summer heat.

C & O **Canal**

1 The C&O Canal Towpath

2 Canoe and kayak rentals

3 Great Falls

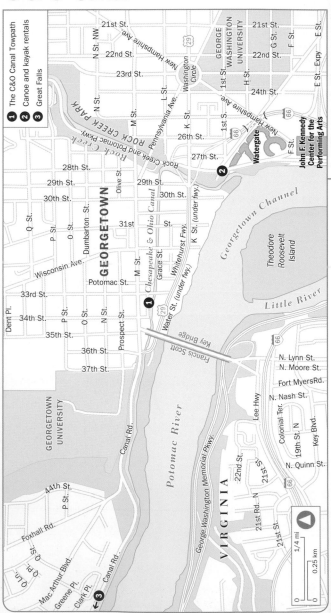

This towpath, along the Chesapeake and Ohio (C&O) Canal, is another stunning natural escape from the bustle of the city. A stretch of tree-lined land curves along the Potomac River at the canal's start in Georgetown, then winds north along the border of West Virginia before ending in Cumberland, Maryland. First opened in 1828 for the purpose of hauling coal between these two ports, the 185-mile (298km) canal and its path are now peopled with leisure joggers, bikers, and power walkers; lovers out for afternoon strolls; campers; and kids. The stunning Potomac River Valley serves as an ever-changing backdrop to all this outdoor activity; summers are gorgeously green, autumn is ablaze in color, and the river itself can be placid or turbulent, but it always makes for prime viewing. START: **The Potomac River, at M or K streets in Georgetown; no Metro access.**

❶ ★ The C & O Canal Tow-path. During milder months, when tourists take over The Mall, you'll find Washingtonians biking, jogging, or walking here en masse, unwinding after a hard week. Start in Georgetown at the western end of K Street (beneath the Whitehurst Fwy.), and then make your way west, following the river. The first few miles are inundated with walkers, so bikers might want to take the parallel Capital Crescent Trail, which is paved and closer to the river. The Capital Crescent trail eventually intersects with the Rock Creek Trail; take the latter for a convenient circular trip of about 22 miles (35k). This trail and the C&O towpath meet near the 3-mile (5k) marker; you can track your progress with regular mile markers along the route. To rent a bike nearby, visit either of these pro shops on M Street: **Revolution Cycles** (3411 M St. NW; ☎ 202/965-3601) or **Bicycle Pro Shop** (3403 M St. NW; ☎ 202/337-0311). Or stop by **Thompson's Boat Center** (at the start of the trail in Georgetown at 2900 Virginia Ave. NW; ☎ 202/333-9543; www.thompsonboatcenter.com), which rents bicycles in addition to canoes and other river-craft. ⏱ *3 hr.*

Chesapeake and Ohio Canal National Historical Park in Georgetown.

Old factories along the Chesapeake and Ohio Canal.

❷ Rent a canoe or kayak.
There are two convenient boat rental centers near the start of the towpath: The aforementioned **Thompson's Boat Center** (2900 Virginia Ave. NW; ☎ 202/333-9543), and **Fletcher's Boathouse** (4940 Canal Rd. NW; ☎ 202/244-0461) at the 3-mile (5k) marker, which is easiest to reach on foot or by bicycle. Both outfits rent kayaks and canoes (Thompson's even offers instructional programs), and Fletcher's has a tackle shop and nearby picnic grounds, too. ⏲ *2 hr.*

❸ ★★★ Explore Great Falls.
A day trip worth taking, this 800-acre (320-hectare) park is known for its scenic beauty, steep gorges, and dramatic waterfalls and rapids, with several overlooks along the river that may take your breath away. It's along the C&O Canal, 14 miles (23km) upriver from Washington in McLean, Virginia, but ambitious bikers can reach it via the towpath. Stop by the Visitor Center for trail maps, park information, and to pick up Junior Ranger booklets if you're traveling with kids. In the summer,

Snacks & Facts

C&O Canal Visitors' Centers are scattered along the route, but only two will likely interest travelers to Washington. The first is in Georgetown (1057 Thomas Jefferson St. NW; ☎ 202/653-5190), near the start of the towpath. It offers historical information and a quick place for a bathroom break. Hungry explorers will find no shortage of food options nearby on K Street, the Washington Harbor, and M Street. The second center is **Great Falls Tavern** (11710 MacArthur Blvd., Potomac, Md.; ☎ 301/767-3714), which provides information, restrooms, and a small snack bar. If you make it to Great Falls, consider stopping at **Old Anglers Inn** (10801 MacArthur Blvd., Potomac, MD; ☎ 301/365-2425; Tues–Sun, lunch and dinner; Mon dinner only), for great New American fare and a fireplace.

Wheels on the Go

Washingtonians know that the Metro and taxis aren't always reliable. For a go-anywhere, do-anything mode of transport in the city, turn to Capital Bikeshare, which has quickly become one of the most popular ways to get around D.C. Sign up for a 24-hour, 3-day, 30-day, or year-long membership, and you'll have more than 3,000 bicycles at your disposal at 350 stations across the city, Virginia, and Maryland. Hop on at one location and return your bike at your destination, no back-tracking required. Membership fees $8 (24 hrs.) to $85 (annual). For more information, visit www.capitalbikeshare.com.

take your family for a ride on a mule-drawn canal boat. Park rangers don period costumes as they operate replica canal boats and share the history of the canal during these trips from Great Falls. **Note**: Ten or more people are required to make a reservation. Otherwise, seats are available at a first come, first-served basis. 🕐 3 hr. On weekends and holidays when the weather's nice, the park is very popular. Get here early (before 10am) to avoid getting stuck in traffic at the entrance gate. Great Falls barge rides: $8 per visitor (ages 15–61), $6 for seniors (ages 62 and up), $5 for children (ages 4–14), kids

age 3 and under ride free. Call Great Falls to confirm boats are running. From D.C. by car: Take Constitution Ave. NW/US-50 to I-66 W/US-50 W. out of the city across Roosevelt Memorial Bridge. Continue until you reach the US-50 W/Arlington Blvd./ GW Pkwy. exit. Turn north onto George Washington Memorial Pkwy (GWMP or GW Pkwy). Follow the GWMP to the exit for I-495 S. When you are on the ramp, stay in the right-hand lane, which will turn into the exit ramp for Rte. 193, Georgetown Pike. Take a left at the traffic light onto Rte. 193 West. In 3 miles, make a right at Old Dominion Dr. to access the park.

Great Falls.

Georgetown

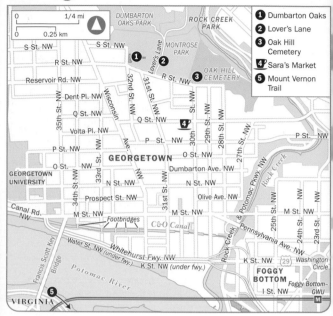

1. Dumbarton Oaks
2. Lover's Lane
3. Oak Hill Cemetery
4. Sara's Market
5. Mount Vernon Trail

The capital's most exclusive neighborhood—with its prize-winning gardens, gargantuan homes, and residents with boldface names out walking their dogs—offers visitors an ideal balance of eye candy and history, best enjoyed under a canopy of trees and blue skies. Tour the parks, stop to smell the flowers, study the statuary, and picnic on the grass with a great bottle of wine. For a walking tour of Georgetown, see p. 88. START: Dumbarton Oaks garden entrance at 31st and R streets in Georgetown; no Metro access.

① ★★ **Dumbarton Oaks.** Enjoy the traditional French, Italian, and English gardens at this once-private home, now open to the public for tours. Discover bubbling fountains, stone archways, romantic hideaways, tiled pools, and even a Roman-style amphitheater. Flora includes an orangery, a rose garden, wisteria-covered arbors, groves of cherry trees, and magnolias. When everything is in bloom, you could spend as long as an hour here. ⏱ 1 hr. 1703 32nd St. NW. ☎ 202/339-6401. www.doaks.org. $10 adults, $8 seniors, $5 children. Gardens: Tues–Sun year-round; Mar 15–Oct 31 2–6pm, Nov 1–Mar 14 2–5pm (except national holidays and Dec 24).

② ★ **Lover's Lane.** Follow the downhill, paved road that hugs Dumbarton Oaks's bricked wall next to Montrose Park. At the bottom, hang to the left and discover a gently cultivated enclave of gurgling brooks, weeping willow trees, wildflowers, and carefully placed benches for maximum romance and relaxation. ⏱ *20 min.*

③ ★ Oak Hill Cemetery. Reminiscent of Europe's historic cemeteries, the iron-gated, hilly grounds here are both beautifully kept and visually breathtaking. Spot a wild fox or a deer among the hundreds of 19th- and 20th-century headstones and the wealth of ornate statuary; stroll down toward the creek on winding paths as you tour yesterday's VIPs—and tell them to RIP. ⏱ *30 min. 30th and R sts. Mon–Fri 9am–4:30pm; Sat 11am–4pm; Sun 1pm–4pm; closed to the public during funerals and on holidays.*

④ Sara's Market. Just off the corner of 30th and Q streets, this sweet, family-owned deli is stocked with upscale treats. Choose from a small selection of prepared sandwiches in the cooler, or grab some British shortcakes, a snack bar, fresh fruit, a bag of nuts, and/or a decent bottle of wine to take with you into the great outdoors. *3008 Q St. NW (at 30th St.).*

Georgetown's Dumbarton Oaks.

Crew teams on the Potomac River overlooking Georgetown

⑤ ★★ Mount Vernon Trail. Just across the river from downtown Georgetown, on Theodore Roosevelt Island, bikers, hikers, and joggers enter this scenic 18-mile (30k) trail. The path hugs the Virginia side of the Potomac River and offers breathtaking views of the classic monuments, memorials, and the river itself. Follow its course over bridges and through parks, and you'll eventually arrive at George Washington's historic Mount Vernon home (p 55). ⏱ *3 hr.* ☎ *703/235-1530. www.nps.gov/gwmp/planyourvisit/mtvernontrail.htm. Metro: Roslyn.*

The Mall & Tidal Basin

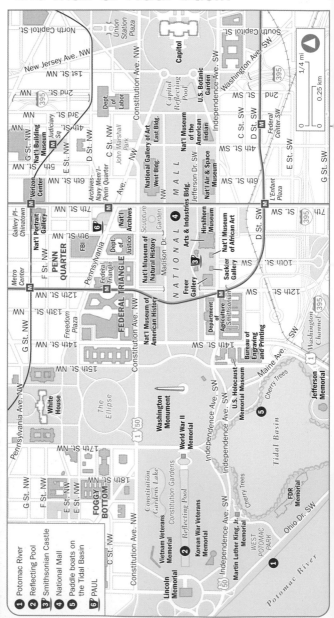

1 Potomac River
2 Reflecting Pool
3 Smithsonian Castle
4 National Mall
5 Paddle boats on the Tidal Basin
6 PAUL

1/4 mil
0.25 km

Before it was the nation's capital, Washington, D.C. was a swamp. And if you wander The Mall and Tidal Basin in July or August, you'll have no trouble imagining what it was like, way back when. But few American urban environments can beat The Mall and Tidal Basin's outdoor appeal in spring, when Japanese cherry blossoms transform the cityscape, or in fall, with its perfect sweater weather. Throw in miles of bike and jogging paths in the heart of the city; botanical gardens; a galloping river; and plenty of green spaces, and you have plenty of reasons for avoiding the indoors. START: **Metro to Smithsonian.**

❶ ★ **kids** **Stroll the Potomac River.** Whether you begin your walk in Georgetown, at Washington Harbor, or head toward the river near the Watergate Hotel or the Lincoln Memorial, spend some time promenading. You'll pass a legion of resident joggers (have you ever seen so many in your life?); admire university crew teams sliding through the water; capture grand glimpses of the memorials, monuments, and bridges from a new perspective; observe historic Georgetown from afar; pass 1 0 or more volleyball games in progress; picnic on the grass with kindred spirits inclined to stop and smell the roses; and root for fishermen who cast their rods in hopes of catching "the big one." On a beautiful day, nothing beats it. ⏱ *1 hr.*

❷ **Reflect at the Reflecting Pool.** Pedestrian paths surround this ⅓-mile-long (.5km) body of water that visually connects the Lincoln Memorial and Washington Monument. It's also the site where thousands gathered to hear Rev. Martin Luther King, Jr., recite his legendary "I Have a Dream" speech in 1963. His followers stood around the pool—and in it—as they listened to the words that would change a nation. ⏱ *20 min.*

❸ ★★ **Smithsonian Castle.** Just off The Mall on Independence Avenue, this is an ideal spot to rest (if your dogs are barking) and to snack (if you're hungry like the wolf). It's also information central for the Smithsonian museums, so grab a sandwich or muffin and pick up a brochure to plan your next adventure. *1000 Jefferson Dr. SW.* ☎ *202/633-1000. www.si.edu. Smithsonian. $–$$.*

❹ ★★★ **kids** **Attend an Event on The Mall.** Depending on the time of year when you arrive in Washington, you may stumble upon ethnic festivals, fireworks, kite-flying celebrations, dance performances, dedication ceremonies,

The reflecting pool.

Cherry Blossoms in Washington

Over 100 years ago in 1912, Tokyo gifted Washington 3,000 delicately flowering, fragrant cherry trees in recognition of the growing friendship between the two cities. In 1965, Tokyo gave D.C. an additional 3,800 trees. Today, an estimated 700,000 travelers from all around the world arrive en masse every March and April, during the peak of the cherry blossom season, to wander amid their riotous color and heady fragrance during the 2-week Cherry Blossom Festival. For a complete schedule of events, visit the official website, www.nationalcherryblossomfestival.org.

children's workshops, orchestra concerts, holiday happenings, and much more on the National Mall. *Check out www.nps.gov/nama to find out what's happening during your visit.*

⑤ ★ kids Rent paddle Boats on the Tidal Basin. Whether you're a kid or just a kid at heart, head to the Tidal Basin, weather permitting, and get ready to exercise your right to see the Jefferson Memorial while working up a sweat. ⏱ *1 hr. 2-passenger boat $15 per hr.; 4-passenger boat $24 per hr. March 15 to Labor Day daily 10am–6pm. Metro: Smithsonian Station*

(Blue/Orange lines; use the 12th St. and Independence Ave. exit). Walk west on Independence toward 15th St. Turn left on Raoul Wallenberg Place/15th St. and continue toward the Jefferson Memorial; look for the Tidal Basin Paddle Boat dock.

⑥ Paul. Order a quiche and a macaron to go at this bustling French bistro and sidewalk café, a Parisian transplant right on Pennsylvania Avenue. *801 Pennsylvania Ave., NW.* ☎ *202/524-4500. www.paul-usa.com. $–$$.* ●

Kite festival on the Mall.

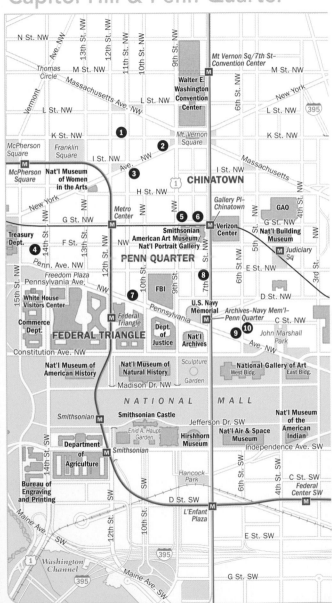

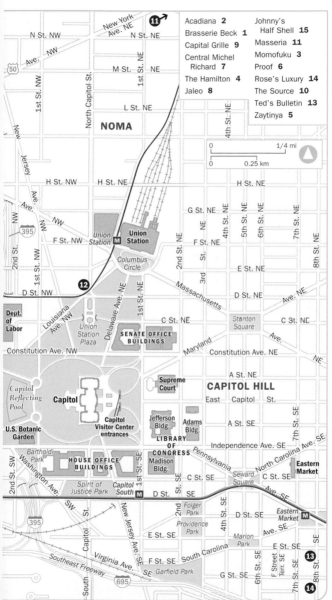

Acadiana **2**
Brasserie Beck **1**
Capital Grille **9**
Central Michel Richard **7**
The Hamilton **4**
Jaleo **8**
Johnny's Half Shell **15**
Masseria **11**
Momofuku **3**
Proof **6**
Rose's Luxury **14**
The Source **10**
Ted's Bulletin **13**
Zaytinya **5**

Georgetown & Dupont Circle

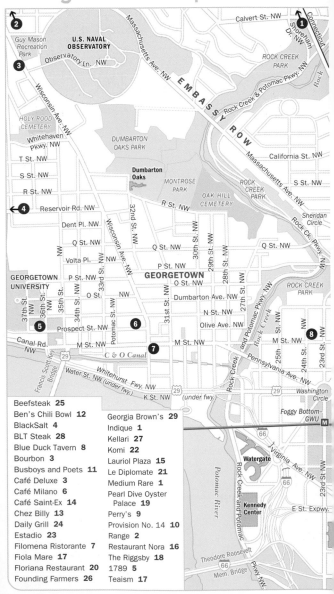

Beefsteak **25**

Ben's Chili Bowl **12**

BlackSalt **4**

BLT Steak **28**

Blue Duck Tavern **8**

Bourbon **3**

Busboys and Poets **11**

Café Deluxe **3**

Café Milano **6**

Café Saint-Ex **14**

Chez Billy **13**

Daily Grill **24**

Estadio **23**

Filomena Ristorante **7**

Fiola Mare **17**

Floriana Restaurant **20**

Founding Farmers **26**

Georgia Brown's **29**

Indique **1**

Kellari **27**

Komi **22**

Lauriol Plaza **15**

Le Diplomate **21**

Medium Rare **1**

Pearl Dive Oyster Palace **19**

Perry's **9**

Provision No. 14 **10**

Range **2**

Restaurant Nora **16**

The Riggsby **18**

1789 **5**

Teaism **17**

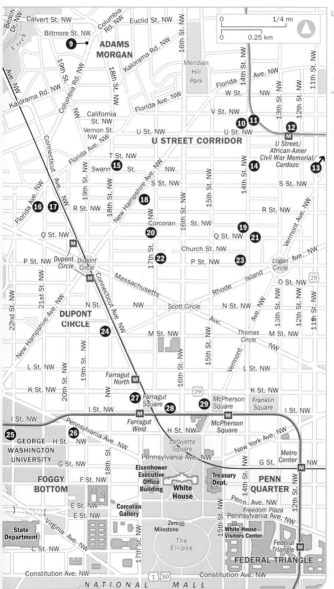

Dining Best Bets

Best Newcomer
★★★ Rose's Luxury $$ 717 8th St. SE *(p 143)*

Best Manhattan Rival
★★★ Momofuku $$ 1090 I St. NW *(p 139)*

Best for Carnivores
★ Medium Rare, $ 3500 Connecticut Ave. NW *(p 139)*

Best Hotel Eats
★★ The Riggsby $$ 1731 New Hampshire Ave. NW *(p 141)*

Best Mussels and Beer
★★ Brasserie Beck $$ 1101 K St. NW *(p 134)*

Best All-Organic
★★ Restaurant Nora $$$ 2132 Florida Ave. NW *(p 141)*

Best Unfussy French
★ Chez Billy $$ 3815 Georgia Ave. NW *(p 136)*

Best Sexy Tapas Place
★★ Estadio $$ 701 9th St. NW *(p 136)*

Best for Flirting with Elected Officials
★★★ The Capital Grille $$$$ 601 Pennsylvania Ave. NW *(p 135)*

Patio seating at Café Milano.

Best for Winos
★★★ Proof $$$ 775 G St. NW *(p 140)*

Best for Blue Bloods
★ Café Milano $$$ 3252 Prospect St. NW *(p 135)*

Best Fireside Dining
★★★ 1789 $$$$ 1226 36th St. NW *(p 141)*

Best Fresh Fish
★★★ Kellari $$$ 1700 K St. NW *(p 139)*

Best for Moody Political Debates
★ Busboys and Poets 2021 14th St. NW *(p 134)*

Best Hipster Joint
★★ Café Saint-Ex $$ 1847 14th St. NW *(p 135)*

Best for Rowdy Rugrats
★★ Café Deluxe $$ 3228 Wisconsin Ave. NW *(p 134)*

Best South of the Border
★ Lauriol Plaza $$ 1835 18th St. NW *(p 139)*

Best Crab Cakes
★ Johnny's Half Shell $$$ 2002 P St. NW *(p 138)*

Best Historic Diner
★ Ben's Chili Bowl $ 1213 U St. NW *(p 133)*

Best Sweet Confections
★★ Ted's Bulletin $ 505 8th St. SE *(p 142)*

Best for Expat Parisians
★★★ Le Diplomate $$ 1601 14th St. NW *(p 139)*

Restaurants A to Z

★★★ **Acadiana** DOWNTOWN
CAJUN New Orleans's legacy is
strong here, in Cajun fare by Jeff
Tunks, who cooked in the Big Easy
for years. Try gumbo with andouille,
crawfish pies, or fried green toma-
toes in this upscale, ornate, but
comfortable setting. *901 New York
Ave. NW (K and 9th sts.).* ☎ *202/
408-8848. www.acadianarestaurant.
com. Entrees $22–$34. AE, DISC,
MC, V. Lunch Mon–Fri; dinner
Mon–Sat. Metro: Mt. Vernon Square.
Map p 128.*

★★ **Beefsteak** DUPONT CIRCLE
AMERICAN Celebrity chef Jose
Andres pushes the produce at this
veggie-centric restaurant, with fare
that features hearty grains, fresh
sauces, and greens. Not completely
vegetarian, it does offer some meat
selections. *800 22nd St. NW.*
☎ *202/296-1421. www.beefsteak
veggies.com. Entrees $6–$9. MC, V.
Daily 10:30am–10pm. Metro: Dupont
Circle. Map p 130.*

★ **Ben's Chili Bowl** U STREET
CORRIDOR *AMERICAN* Known
for its Formica tables, sloppy chili
dogs and late-night banter, this
old-time diner has drawn a who's
who of influential African-Americans
since 1958—from Martin Luther
King, Jr. to Redd Foxx, and Barack
Obama. *1213 U St. NW (at 12th St.).*
☎ *202/667-0909. www.benschili
bowl.com. Entrees $10. No credit
cards. Mon–Sat breakfast, lunch &
dinner; Sun lunch, dinner. Metro: U
St./Cardozo Map p 130.*

★★★ **Black Salt** PALISADES
SEAFOOD Local seafood fans
rave for chef Jeff Black's D.C.
catch—this restaurant and fish market, with perfectly cooked black sea
bass, fried Ipswich clams, fish stews,
and more. *4883 MacArthur Blvd. NW
(at V St.).* ☎ *202/342-9101. www.
blacksaltrestaurant.com. Entrees
$33–$38. DC, DISC, MC, V. Lunch
Mon–Sat; dinner daily. No Metro
access. Bus: B6. Map p 130.*

★ **BLT Steak** DOWNTOWN
AMERICAN The D.C. outpost of
this upscale chain serves quality
steak with different sauces, and fish
from the raw bar. The chef's warm
popovers are just right. *1625 I St.
NW.* ☎ *202/689-8999. www.blt
steak.com. Entrees $29–$59. AE,
DISC, MC, V. Lunch Mon–Fri, dinner
Mon–Sat. Metro: Farragut West. Map
p 130.*

★★ **Blue Duck Tavern** DOWN-
TOWN *AMERICAN* This downtown restaurant's comfortable
American feel—hand-carved
wooden benches and chairs, an
inviting open kitchen, and a stellar
menu—keeps Washingtonians coming back. *24th and M Sts. NW.*
☎ *202/419-6755. www.blueduck
tavern.com. Entrees $15–$36. AE,
DISC, MC, V. Breakfast daily; brunch
Sat–Sun; lunch Mon–Fri; dinner daily.
Metro: Foggy Bottom or Farragut
North. Map p 130.*

*Don't let the name fool you: Veggies take
center stage at Beefsteak.*

Brasserie Beck.

★ **kids** **Bourbon** ADAMS MORGAN *AMERICAN* Young 20-somethings and families flock to this consistently good restaurant for tater tots, burgers, and bourbon BBQ. *2321 18th St. NW.* ☎ *202/332-0800. www.bourbondc. com. Entrees $8–$20. AE, DISC, MC, V. Brunch Sundays only; dinner daily. Metro: Dupont Circle. Map p 130.*

★★ **Brasserie Beck** DOWNTOWN *BELGIAN* Skip the trip to Europe and head to this Belgian bistro for authentic brews and dishes such as steamed mussels, seared scallops, crispy chicken, and more than 50 beers. *1101 K St. NW.* ☎ *202/408-1717. www.beckdc.com. Entrees $23–$37. AE, DISC, MC, V. Lunch Mon–Fri, dinner daily; brunch Sat–Sun. Metro: Metro Center. Map p 130.*

★ **kids** **Busboys & Poets** 14TH STREET/LOGAN CIRCLE *AMERICAN* Local lit majors, groovy families, and budget fashionistas flock here for pizzas, burgers, and sandwiches, artfully prepared and affordable. *2021 14th St. NW (V St.).* ☎ *202/387-POET [7638]. www.bus boysandpoets.com. Entrees $12–$26. AE, DC, DISC, MC, V. Breakfast, lunch and dinner daily. Metro: U St./ Cardozo Map p 130.*

★★ **kids** **Café Deluxe** CATHEDRAL *AMERICAN* Can one bistro really serve all? Seems this one does: Guys hang out at the bar and watch sports. Families come early for the kids menu and buckets of crayons. Foodies swear by the tuna steak sandwich. Young lovers sip cocktails and gaze at each other. Everyone else simply enjoys the solid New American fare. *3228*

Eating Out with Kids

Restaurant hopping with the family in tow can be overwhelming, but these venues around the city make it easy. So sit back, let the kids be kids, and relax: No waiter will give you the stink-eye here. Inventive salads, burgers, crab cakes, and a kids' menu keep everyone happy at **Chef Geoff's** (3201 New Mexico Ave., NW. ☎ 202/237-7800) in American University Park. Best of all: A spacious outdoor porch set off from the road for al fresco dining with little ones. Tots color on the papered tables at **Cafe Deluxe** (3228 Wisconsin Ave., NW. ☎ 202/686-2233), while adults sip wine and enjoy everything from meatloaf to grilled ahi tuna at this casual eatery close to the National Cathedral. Kids getting antsy? Then head to **Comet Ping Pong** (5037 Connecticut Ave., NW. ☎ 202/364-0404), a restaurant with ping pong tables in the back. Pizzas are simple and tasty, but it's the atmosphere that will drive you here.

Gather around a cozy table to share authentic Spanish tapas at Estadio.

Wisconsin Ave. NW (at Macomb St.).
☎ 202/686-2233. www.cafedeluxe.
com. Entrees $12–$24. AE, MC, V.
Lunch Mon–Thurs & Sun; dinner Mon–
Sun. No Metro access. Map p 130.

★ **Café Milano** GEORGETOWN
ITALIAN Pushy lobbyists, the society set, smug playboys, and ambitious young women in skimpy
dresses don't flock here for the
decent, but unremarkable, Italian
food. They do come here to make
the scene, close a deal, drink too
much, touch the hems of power,
and let loose, Washington-style, at
this supercharged, always-packed
restaurant and lounge. 3251 Prospect St. NW (at M St.). ☎ 202/333-
6183. www.cafemilano.com. Entrees
$35–$65. AE, DC, DISC, MC, V.
Lunch & dinner daily. Metro: Foggy
Bottom or Roslyn. Map p 130.

★★ **Café Saint-Ex** 14TH
STREET/U STREET CORRIDOR
AMERICAN This Eurochic bar and
bistro attracts the young and hip
for New American fare. A DJ spins
in the lounge. 1847 14th St. NW (T
St.). ☎ 202/265-7839. www.saint-ex.
com. Entrees $15–$29. AE, DISC,
MC, V. Dinner daily; Brunch Sat–Sun.
Metro: U St./Cardozo Map p 130.

★★★ **Capital Grille** PENN
QUARTER *AMERICAN* Cut
through the throng of short-skirted
interns and married officials at the

bar, and dig into juicy steak over
gossip from power players talking
too loudly at nearby tables. 601
Pennsylvania Ave. NW (6th St.).
☎ 202/737-6200. www.capitalgrille.
com. Entrees $29–$52. AE, DC, DISC,
MC, V. Lunch Mon–Sat; dinner daily.
Metro: Archives/Navy Memorial.
Map p 128.

★★ **Central Michel Richard**
DOWNTOWN *AMERICAN/
FRENCH* Chef Michel Richard
dishes out unstuffy fare such as
French onion soup, mussels, lobster
burgers, and soft shell crab. 1001
Pennsylvania Ave. NW. ☎ 202/626-
0015. www.centralmichelrichard.com.
Entrees $24–$35. Lunch Mon–Fri; din-
ner daily. Metro: Federal Triangle.
Map p 128.

Central Michael Richard.

★ **Chez Billy** PETWORTH *FRENCH* "Chez" may make it sound fancy, but nothing is pretentious in this unfussy neighborhood bistro. Instead, you'll find good French fare, a lively atmosphere and fun cocktails. *3815 Georgia Ave. NW.* ☎ *202/506-2080. www.chez billy.com. Entrees $17–$28. AE, MC, V. Dinner daily; brunch Sun. Metro: Georgia Avenue. Map p 130.*

★★ kids **Daily Grill** DUPONT CIRCLE *AMERICAN* With several locations, this Washington staple is perfect for a quick lunch or dinner with kids, whether you're craving a burger and fries or seared salmon and baked potato. You'll find roomy booths and an after-work bar scene. *1200 18th St. NW (Connecticut Ave.).* ☎ *202/822-5282. www.dailygrill. com. Entrees $16–$30. AE, DC, DISC, MC, V. Lunch & dinner daily; brunch Sat–Sun. Metro: Dupont Circle. Map p 130.*

★★ **Estadio** 14TH STREET *SPAN-ISH* D.C. has no shortage of tapas restaurants, but this one stands out for its top-notch twists on Spanish cuisine like *tortilla española* with its creamy egg and peppers or the sautéed chorizo picante. *1520 14th St. NW. 202/319-1404. www.*

estadio-dc.com. Tapas $5–$12. AE, DISC, MC, V. Lunch Fri; Dinner daily; Brunch Sun. Metro: Dupont Circle. Map p 130.

★★ **Filomena Ristorante** GEORGETOWN *ITALIAN* Washington Harbour has loads of restaurants but nothing beats this funky Italian spot a short walk from the waterfront. The interior is adorned with tacky decorations, doilies, and a zany assortment of seasonal items, but the wine list is great and so is the traditional Italian feel, down to the cook rolling handmade pasta upstairs. The bowls of pasta are recommended for those who want a true Italian meal. It's casual enough that you won't need to dress up for dinner, but elegant enough that you shouldn't wear shorts. Come hungry: Portions are enough for two. Book your table in advance, especially on weekend nights. *1063 Wisconsin Ave. NW.* ☎ *202/338-8800. www.filomena. com. Entrees $22–$42. AE, DISC, MC, V. Lunch & dinner daily. No Metro access. Map p 130.*

★★ **Fiola Mare** GEORGETOWN *SEAFOOD* Enjoy the view from this glass-walled restaurant along the Georgetown waterfront and

Enjoy the views from Fiola Mare Kennedy Lounge on the Potomac River.

Sandwiches at Founding Farmers Restaurant.

feast on a menu of sustainable seafood that changes seasonally. *3050 K St. NW (Enter at 31st St & Waterfront).* ☎ *202/628-0065. www.fiolamaredc.com. Entrees $24–$44. AE, DISC, MC, V. Lunch Tues–Fri; Dinner daily. No Metro access. Map p 130.*

★ **Floriana Restaurant** DUPONT CIRCLE *ITALIAN* Tucked away in a historic Dupont town house, this restaurant makes you feel as if you're dining in someone's very nice living room. It features some of the best Italian in the city, too: Think butternut squash ravioli and truffle risotto. *1602 17th St. NW.* ☎ ☎ *202/667-5937. www.floriana restaurant.com. Entrees $15–$34. AE, MC, V. Dinner daily; brunch Sat–Sun. Metro: Dupont Circle. Map p 130.*

★ **Founding Farmers** DOWNTOWN *AMERICAN* True to its name, this restaurant celebrates the American farmer, serving sustainably farmed, grown, and harvested foods. The heartland-inspired menu rotates seasonally, depending on what's available. *1924 Pennsylvania Ave. NW.* ☎ *202/822-8783. www. wearefoundingfarmers.com. Entrees $20–$30. Lunch & dinner daily; breakfast Mon–Fri; brunch Sat–Sun. Metro: Farragut West or Foggy Bottom. Map p 130.*

Georgia Brown's DOWNTOWN *SOUTHERN* The dining room may seem formal, but the food is fit for a down-home, Southern jubilee: golden-fried chicken; cornmeal-crusted catfish fingers; shrimp and grits; and sweet, crunchy fried okra. *950 15th St. NW (at K St.).* ☎ *202/393-4499. www.gbrowns. com. Entrees $21–$35. AE, DC, DISC, MC, V. Lunch and dinner daily; brunch Sun. Metro: Farragut North. Map p 130.*

★ **The Hamilton** DOWNTOWN *AMERICAN* A favorite of downtown lunch goers, this restaurant is massive (400 seats) and so is its menu, offering everything from sushi to sliders. A live music venue downstairs offers regular nightly

The Hamilton.

A Seat at the Bar

Most D.C. restaurants require reservations, and in this cutthroat town, all of the best seem always to be booked. What's a hungry, reservation-less foodie to do? Head to the bar, of course. In an effort to please those who haven't managed to reserve a table in their main dining rooms, but who nevertheless hope to sample some of their food, a number of the city's top restaurants serve either their full menu or a modified version of it at the bar. The experience often proves more intimate and convivial than that in the main dining room, and here's the kicker: It's always less expensive.

–Elise Hartman Ford

shows. *14th and F sts. NW.* ☎ *202/787-1000. www.thehamiltondc.com. Entrees $17–$29. AE, DC, DISC, MC, V. Lunch, dinner, and late-night daily. Metro: Metro Center. Map p 130.*

★ **Indique** CLEVELAND PARK *INDIAN* Curry, naan, biriyani. All of the flavors of India are here at this chic two-floor restaurant known for its consistently good fare. *3512 Connecticut Ave. NW.* ☎ *202/244-6600. www.indique.com. Lunch Fri–Sun; dinner daily. $14–$19. AE, DC, DISC, MC, V. Metro: Cleveland Park. Map p 130.*

★ **Jaleo** PENN QUARTER *SPANISH* Chef José Andrés started the "small plates" revolution in

Gambas al Ajillo at Jaleo.

Washington with this sexy, casual tapas bar and restaurant in the heart of Penn Quarter. *480 7th St. NW (at E St.).* ☎ *202/628-7949. www.jaleo.com. Entrees $15–$26, tapas $8–$16. AE, DC, DISC, MC, V. Lunch & dinner daily; brunch Sat–Sun. Metro: Gallery Place/Chinatown. Map p 128.*

Travel Tip

If a place beckons, call ahead for reservations, especially on a Saturday night. You can often reserve your table online at www.opentable.com. If you wait until the last minute to make a reservation, expect to dine early or very late— say 5:30 to 6pm or after 9:30pm.

★ **kids Johnny's Half Shell** CAPITOL HILL *SEAFOOD* Maryland is famous for its crab cakes, and this small, no-frills neighborhood restaurant cooks them with loads of meat and very little filler. Casual and kid-friendly. *400 N. Capitol St., NW (at Louisiana Ave).* ☎ *202/737-0400. www.johnnyshalfshell.net. Entrees $18–$40. AE, MC, V. Lunch Mon–Fri; dinner Mon–Sat. Metro: Union Station. Map p 128.*

★★★ Kellari DOWNTOWN

GREEK   Prepare for an expensive dinner here, but it will be worth it, especially if you handpick your fresh fish, which has been flown in from Spain or Greece that day. *Spanakopita* and *saganaki,* the traditional flaming Graviera cheese, are the real deal at this tavern. *1700 K St. NW.* ☎ *202/535-5274. www. kellaridc.com. Entrees $25 and up. AE, MC, V. Lunch & dinner daily; brunch Sat–Sun. Metro: Farragut North. Map p 130.*

★★ Komi DUPONT CIRCLE

AMERICAN   Chef Johnny Monis's savory Mediterranean cooking, homemade breads, and light, lively desserts will wow you. The tiny dining room is casual, the service perfect. Worth the wait. *1509 17th St. NW (near P St.).* ☎ *202/332-9200. www.komirestaurant.com. Tasting menu $150 per person; wine pairing $75. AE, MC, V. Dinner Tues–Sat. Metro: Dupont Circle. Map p 130.*

★ Lauriol Plaza DUPONT CIRCLE

MEXICAN   Is this multilevel place ever not packed to the roof, where singles flirt and drink? The Mexican fare is worth its salt—as are the strong margaritas. *1835 18th St. NW (at S St.).* ☎ *202/387-0035. www. lauriolplaza.com. Entrees $6.50–$16. AE, DC, DISC, MC, V. Lunch & dinner daily. Metro: Dupont Circle. Map p 130.*

★★★ Le Diplomate. 14TH

STREET *FRENCH*   When this casual French bistro first opened, foodies waited up to 2 months for a reservation. Thankfully, it's a *little* easier to get a seat here now. Diners feast on traditional French classics: duck confit, onion soup gratinée, escargots, and Bouillabaisse. *1601 14th St. NW.* ☎ *202/332-3333. www.lediplomatedc.com. Entrees $17–$35. AE, MC, V. Dinner daily; brunch, Sat–Sun;* mid-day (3pm–5pm) Sat–Sun. Metro: Dupont Circle. Map p 130.

★ Masseria UNION MARKET

ITALIAN   Choose from three- and five-course menus featuring fish, meat, and pasta at this secluded Italian restaurant in D.C.'s newly developed Union Market area. Take a seat on the large front patio to sip cocktails and snack on small plates during happy hour. *1340 4th St. NE.* ☎ *202/608-1330. www. masseria-dc.com. 3 courses at $62 or 5 courses at $84. Metro: NOMA/ Galludet. Map p 128.*

★ Medium Rare CLEVELAND

PARK *AMERICAN*   Meat lovers, this one's for you. This restaurant offers a prix-fixe menu of the best steak and frites in town with their tasty "secret sauce." You also get bread and a side salad. *3500 Connecticut Ave. NW.* ☎ *202/237-1432. www.mediumrarerestaurant.com. Prix-fixe $21. AE, DISC, MC, V. Dinner daily; brunch Sat–Sun. Metro: Cleveland Park Map p 130.*

★★★ Momofuku/Milk Bar

DOWNTOWN *ASIAN*   Young chef David Chang brings his New York blockbuster to D.C., serving a

The outside pergola at Masseria.

revolving menu of Asian dishes from noodles to Korean fish and rice cakes to Kimchi stew. *1090 I St. NW. 202/602-1832. www.momofuku. com/dc/ccdc. $14–$25. AE, MC, V. Dinner daily; lunch Mon–Fri. Metro: Metro Center or McPherson Square. Map p. 128.*

★★ Pearl Dive Oyster Palace

14TH STREET *SEAFOOD* Fan of Old Black Salts or Cedar Islands? You'll find a large selection of oysters here—served hot or on ice—along with a variety of seafood dishes. Sit at the sidewalk oyster bar or enjoy a drink at the Black Jack bar upstairs while you wait for a table. *1612 14th St. NW. ☎ 202/319-1612. www.pearldivedc. com. Entrees $22–$27. AE, MC, V. Dinner daily; brunch Fri–Sun. Metro: Dupont Circle. Map p 130.*

★★ Perry's ADAMS MORGAN

JAPANESE With one of the busiest rooftop scenes in the city, Perry's has been long famous for its Sunday drag brunch. Everyone from GW students to 40-somethings collide here for solid Japanese fare. *1811 Columbia Rd. NW. ☎ 202/234-6218. www.perrysadamsmorgan.com. Brunch Sun; lunch Sat; dinner daily. Entrees $17–$42. AE, DISC, MC, V.*

Metro: Woodley Park-Zoo/Adams Morgan. Map p 130.

★★★ Proof PENN QUARTER

AMERICAN Choose from some 1,000 bottles of wine, then dine on freshly prepared contemporary dishes that make a nod toward eco-friendly cuisine. *775 G St. NW. ☎ 202/737-7663. www.proofdc. com. Entrees $25–$35. AE, MC, V. Lunch Tues–Fri, dinner daily. Metro: Gallery Place/Chinatown. Map p 128.*

★ Provision 14 14TH STREET

AMERICAN Young professionals flock here after work for the lively bar scene and big batch cocktails, along with the communal-style small and large plates, such as chili-braised short ribs and Maryland scallops. *2100 14th St. NW. ☎ 202/827-4530. www.provisiondc. com. $12–$42. AE, MC, V. Dinner daily; brunch Sat–Sun. Metro: U St./ Cardozo. Map p 130.*

★ Range FRIENDSHIP HEIGHTS

AMERICAN Top chef Bryan Voltaggio presents a "range" of good American eats at this contemporary restaurant where wood-fired meat and chicken are carefully prepared in an open kitchen. *5335 Wisconsin Ave. NW. (Chevy Chase Pavilion, 2nd Floor) ☎ 202/803-8020. www.*

The Riggsby, in the Carlyle Hotel.

Mobile Eats

One can say many things about Washington, but one thing is definitely true: When we find something we like, we stick to it. The trend in food trucks serving a variety of ethnic and healthy tastes is no exception. Keep an eye out for Phonation, which serves up delicious pho and banh mi. You'll find sweet and savory pie slices at DCPieTruck, the roving counterpart of local pie shop Dangerously Delicious Pies on H Street. And as the name implies, the Red Hook Lobster Pound truck dishes out delicious Maine-style lobster rolls for $16. Track them all via Twitter or visit www.foodtruckfiesta.com to find their current locations.

voltrange.com. AE, MC, V. Dinner daily; lunch Sat–Sun. Metro: Friendship Heights. Map p 130.

★★ **Restaurant Nora** DUPONT CIRCLE *ORGANIC* An early advocate of fresh, seasonal ingredients, chef-owner Nora Pouillon serves up dishes like free-range chicken and tender roasted pork that are testament to how good a simple, organic meal can be. Great wine list. *2132 Florida Ave. NW (at R St.).* ☎ *202/462-5143. www.noras.com. Entrees $29–402. AE, MC, V. Dinner Mon–Sat. Metro: Dupont Circle. Map p 130.*

★★ **The Riggsby** DUPONT CIRCLE AMERICAN Recalling Old Hollywood in design, this restaurant in the glamorous Carlyle Hotel has it all: crispy chicken, scallops, chopped salads, and even tater tots. *1731 New Hampshire Ave. NW.* ☎ *202/787-1500. www.theriggsby.com. Entrees $16–$38. AE, MC, V. Breakfast, lunch and dinner daily. Metro: Dupont Circle. Map p 130.*

★★★ **Rose's Luxury** CAPITOL HILL AMERICAN The line can stretch around the block to get into this neighborhood hotspot where chef/owner Aaron Silverman takes pride in his small, but impressive

menu of innovative American plates. No reservations for groups under 6. *717 8th St. SE.* ☎ *202/580-8889. www.rosesluxury.com. $12–$16. AE, MC, V. Dinner Mon–Sat. Metro: Eastern Market. Map p 128.*

★★★ **1789** GEORGETOWN *AMERICAN* Go for the feel of old money, antiques, and old-fashioned service—plus romantic lighting and a fireplace on cold nights. The quintessential Georgetown experience, serving new American fare and fabulous wines. *1226 36th St. NW (at Prospect St.).* ☎ *202/965-1789. www.1789restaurant.com.*

Chefs planning a meal at Rose's Luxury.

Dining under the trees at Zaytinya.

Entrees $28–$46. AE, DC, DISC, MC, V. Dinner daily. No Metro access. Bus: DC Circulator. Map p 130.

★★ Sonoma Restaurant and Wine Bar CAPITOL HILL *AMERICAN* Oenophiles and fans of simply prepared, New American fare will adore Sonoma. With 40-plus wines by the glass, plus a lovingly edited wine list of 100 Californian-Italian and French bottles, this upscale but casual bistro is the perfect place to sit and unwind after a long day of sightseeing while nibbling on small plates. *223 Pennsylvania Ave. SE.* ☎ *202/544-8088. www.sonomadc.com. Small plates $12–$14; entrees $12–$28. Lunch Mon–Fri; dinner daily. Metro: Capitol South.*

★★★ The Source DOWNTOWN *ASIAN-AMERICAN* Wolfgang Puck made his D.C. debut with this Asian-Fusion restaurant in the Newseum. Guests sample dishes such as stir-fried lobster or whole roasted duckling for two in an airy, modern space. *575 Pennsylvania Ave. NW.* ☎ *202/637-6100. www.wolfgangpuck.com. Entrees $26–$45. Lunch Mon–Fri, dinner Mon–Sat. Metro: Archives/Penn Quarter. Map p 128.*

kids Teaism DUPONT CIRCLE *ASIAN* Eavesdrop on moody

political debates inside as you sup on healthy noodle dishes and baked goods. *2009 R St. NW (Connecticut Ave. and 21st St.).* ☎ *202/667-3827. www.teaism.com. Entrees $2–$14. AE, MC, V. Breakfast, lunch & dinner daily. Metro: Dupont Circle. Map p 130.*

★★ Ted's Bulletin CAPITOL HILL *AMERICAN* Extra, extra! Read all about it at this fun Barrack's Row restaurant that features newspapers for menus and some of the city's best comfort food. Don't leave without trying one of their famous milkshakes or pop tarts. (Also, now on 14th St. NW). *505 8th St. NW.* ☎ *202/544-8337. www.tedsbulletin.com. Entrees $15–$25. AE, MC, V. Breakfast, lunch, and dinner daily. Metro: Eastern Market. Map p 128.*

★★★ Zaytinya PENN QUARTER *MIDDLE EASTERN* Zaytinya is a must for fans of tapas-style dining—with its soaring ceilings, white-washed walls, communal tables shared by beautiful people, and modern Middle Eastern mezze. *701 9th St. NW (at G St.).* ☎ *202/638-0800. www.zaytinya.com. Entrees $9–$23. AE, DC, DISC, MC, V. Lunch & dinner daily. Metro: Gallery Place/Chinatown. Map p 128.* ●

The Best **Nightlife**

D.C. Nightlife

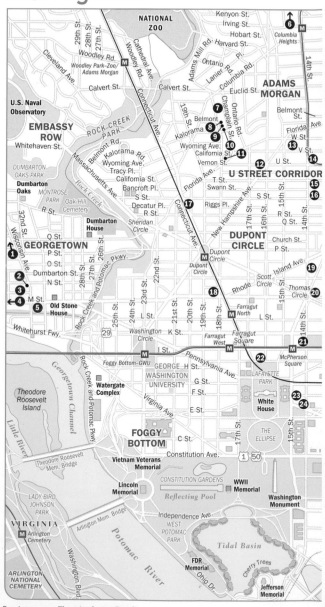

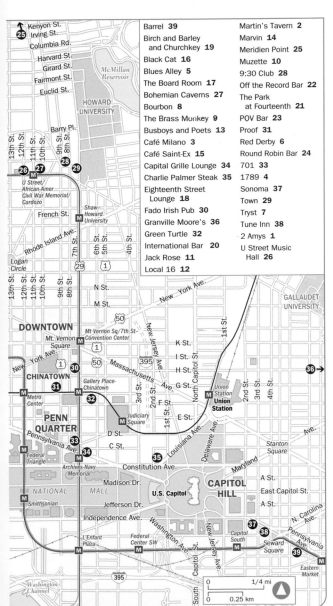

Barrel **39**

Birch and Barley and Churchkey **19**

Black Cat **16**

Blues Alley **5**

The Board Room **17**

Bohemian Caverns **27**

Bourbon **8**

The Brass Monkey **9**

Busboys and Poets **13**

Café Milano **3**

Café Saint-Ex **15**

Capital Grille Lounge **34**

Charlie Palmer Steak **35**

Eighteenth Street Lounge **18**

Fado Irish Pub **30**

Granville Moore's **36**

Green Turtle **32**

International Bar **20**

Jack Rose **11**

Local 16 **12**

Martin's Tavern **2**

Marvin **14**

Meridien Point **25**

Muzette **10**

9:30 Club **28**

Off the Record Bar **22**

The Park at Fourteenth **21**

POV Bar **23**

Proof **31**

Red Derby **6**

Round Robin Bar **24**

701 **33**

1789 **4**

Sonoma **37**

Town **29**

Tryst **7**

Tune Inn **38**

2 Amys **1**

U Street Music Hall **26**

Nightlife Best Bets

Best for **Hopheads**
★★ Churchkey, *1337 14th St. NW (p 147)*

Best for Watching Interns **Flirt with Elected Officials**
★ Charlie Palmer Steak, *101 Constitution Ave. NW (p 151)*

Best for **Rubbing Shoulders with Capitol Hillers**
★ Tune Inn, *331 Pennsylvania Ave. SE (p 151)*

Best for **Wine & Romance**
★★★ 1789, *1226 36th St. NW (p 152)*

Best for Overhearing **State Secrets**
★★ Off the Record Bar, *Hay Adams Hotel, 800 16th St. NW (p 151)*

Best for **Scotch Lovers**
★ Barrel, *613 Pennsylvania Ave. SE (p 152)*

Best for **Live Jazz & Blues**
★ Blues Alley, *1073 Wisconsin Ave. NW (p 149)*

Best for Catching **Indie Acts**
★ 9:30 Club, *815 V St. NW (p 150)*

Best for **Drinks** While the Kids Eat **Pizza**
★★ 2 Amys, *3715 Macomb St. NW (p 148)*

Best for Mingling with **Socialites**
★ Café Milano, *3252 Prospect St. NW (p 151)*

Best **Literary/Artsy-Fartsy Haunt**
★ Busboys and Poets, *2021 14th St. NW (p 148)*

Best for Getting **Your Groove On**
U Street Music Hall, *1115 U St. NW (p 152)*

Best **Al Fresco Ambiance**
★★ Poolside at the International Bar, *Washington Plaza Hotel, 10 Thomas Circle NW (p 150)*

Best for **Monumental Views**
★ POV Bar, *W Hotel, 515 15th St. NW (p 150)*

Best **Rooftop Drinking**
Local 16, *1602 U St. NW (p 150)*

Best **Dive Bar**
★ Red Derby, *3718 14th St. NW (p 149)*

Best for **Grapeheads**
★★ Proof, *775 G St., NW (p 152)*

Travel Tip

Metro trains run until 3am on weekends, and the D.C. Circulator goes to Adams Morgan (home to lots of clubs, but no Metro stops). Take the Metro to the Red Line's Woodley Park–Zoo/Adams Morgan station, and hop on the D.C. Circulator's Green Line to Adams Morgan, which stops at 18th St. NW, Columbia Rd. NW, and then heads south on 14th Street. The shuttle runs Sunday through Thursday from 7am to midnight, and Friday and Saturday from 7am to 3:30am. The fare is $1. Visit www.dccirculator.com for more information.

Nightlife A to Z

Birch and Barley and Churchkey is a must-stop for beer lovers.

Beer Lovers/Casual

★★ Birch and Barley and Churchkey 14TH STREET   A multilevel bar/restaurant and a selection of more than 50 drafts plus more than 600 bottles make this spot a brew lover's paradise. *1337 14th St. NW.* ☎ *202/567-2576. www.birchandbarley.com. Metro: Dupont Circle*

★ Fado Irish Pub PENN QUARTER   This authentic Irish watering hole has a true taste of the Emerald Isle, from vintage tables and chairs to the huge stones that make up the walls and floors, plus pints of Guinness on tap. The din here is at 10 decibels, the pub grub is savory, and the music is live. *808 7th St. NW (at H St.).* ☎ *202/789-0066. www.fadoirishpub.com. Metro: Gallery Place/Chinatown.*

Granville Moore's H STREET   You'll find more than 100 imports at this gastropub, but check the blackboard before you order; things change daily. Visit during happy hour (Sun–Thurs) and beers from D.C., Maryland, and Virginia are only $6. Don't forget to order mussels and frites with your beer. *1238 H St. NE.* ☎ *202/399-2546. www. granvillemoores.com. Metro: Union Station, then a 10-min. walk.*

Meridian Pint COLUMBIA HEIGHTS   This bar is dedicated to American craft beers, so Belgian beer lovers won't find anything here. But the list of drafts and bottles is 60-plus long, and updated daily online. Flat screens and arcade games add to the fun. *3400 11th St., NW.* ☎ *202/588-1075. www.meridianpint.com. Metro: Columbia Heights.*

★ Jack Rose Dining Saloon ADAMS MORGAN   Beer is serious business here, and poured from a hand-built, 20-line, surgical-grade stainless steel draft system. There's lots to choose from off the draft list, but don't be shy about asking for off-menu brews either. *2007 18th St. NW.* ☎ *202/588-7388. www.jack rosediningsaloon.com. Metro: Dupont Circle*

Pizzas at 2 Amys.

Family Spirits
★★ 2 Amys GLOVER PARK
Mom and Dad, you need a drink, and the rugrats are hungry. So take them out for authentic Neapolitan pizza while you savor a lovely glass of Italian red wine. *3715 Macomb St. NW (at Wisconsin Ave.).* ☎ *202/885-5700. www.2amyspizza.com. Metro: Tenleytown/AU.*

Gay & Lesbian
★ Town U STREET CORRIDOR
Wild nights are the norm at this high-energy dance club that has an outside smoking area, two levels, and video screens, and stays open until 4am. *2009 8th St. NW.* ☎ *202/234-TOWN. www.towndc.com. Cover $10–$15. Metro: U Street/Cardozo.*

Hipster Haunts
Board Room. DOWNTOWN   Up for a game of Hungry Hungry Hippo? Or Mousetrap? Rent them for cheap and get your game on. Beer, wine and cocktails are on tap here, but there's no kitchen, so either bring your own food or order in and have it delivered for free. *1737 Connecticut Ave. NW.* ☎ *202/518-7666. www.boardroomdc.com. Metro: Farragut North.*

★ Busboys and Poets 14TH STREET   Local lit majors and broke fashionistas flock here for pizzas, burgers, and booze. Prices won't break the bank. *2021 14th St. NW (at U St.).* ☎ *202/387-7638. www.busboysandpoets.com. AE, MC, V. Metro: U St./Cardozo*

Café Saint-Ex 14TH STREET
Named for the author of *Le Petit Prince,* this Eurochic bar and bistro attracts goateed hipsters and their supercilious dates for New American fare. A DJ spins in the downstairs lounge. *1847 14th St. NW (at T*

Stop by Busboys and Poets for dinner and drinks that won't bust your budget.

St.). ☎ 202/265-7839. www.saint-ex. com Metro: U St./Cardozo

★ **Marvin** 14TH STREET Join locals on the upstairs deck to mingle, discuss politics, and drink a selection of craft beers. *2007 14th St. NW (at U St.) 202/797-7171. www.marvindc.com. AE, MC, V. Metro: U St./Cardozo.*

★ **Passenger** SHAW This newly reopened hipster haunt has a rooftop deck and larger space, but the same eclectic cocktail menu featuring fresh herbs and different liquors, outlined on a chalkboard above the bar each day. *1539 7th St. NW. ☎ 202/393-0220. www.passengerdc.com. Metro: Shaw/Howard.*

★ **Red Derby** COLUMBIA HEIGHTS Seriously unpretentious and dive bar-esque, Red Derby is the place to go for a can of PBR and nachos. Its Sunday brunch packs the house. *3718 14th St. NW. ☎ 202/291-5000. www.redderby. com. Metro: Columbia Heights.*

Tryst ADAMS MORGAN Part coffee house, part playground, part gallery, part pick-up lounge, and part study hall, Tryst is all things for most Adams Morganers. Early to open and late to close, this always buzzing gathering spot is the spot to ogle original art, eat a sandwich, score a scone, groove to live music, or journal furiously while downing an English ale. *2459 18th St. NW (at Columbia Rd.) ☎ 202/232-5500. www.trystdc.com. Mon–Thurs 6:30am–midnight, Fri–Sat 6:30am–2am, Sun 7am–midnight. Metro: Woodley Park–Zoo/Adams Morgan.*

Karaoke

★★ **The Brass Monkey** ADAMS MORGAN If you like singing for your supper or belting out a good '80s tune, look no further than this local dive that offers karaoke on the bottom floor. *2317 18th St. NW.*

☎ 202/265-6665. Metro: Woodley Park–Zoo/Adams Morgan.

★★ **Muzette** ADAMS MORGAN Those who only want to embarrass themselves in front of friends and not a bar full of strangers should rent a room at Muzette. You'll find a great song selection and tasty Korean dishes to accompany your solo act. *2305 18th St. NW (btw. N. Kalorama and N. Belmont Rd.) ☎ 202/758-2971. www.muzette. com. Metro: Adams Morgan.*

Live Music

★★ **Black Cat** 14th STREET Faded punk rockers, still riding on the Sex Pistols' glory days, gather here to vet a new generation of mohawked wonders, and to check out other national and international alternative acts. *1811 14th St. NW (between S and T sts.). ☎ 202/667-4490. www.blackcatdc.com. Metro: U St./Cardozo.*

★ **Blues Alley** GEORGETOWN The *New York Times* once called this place "the nation's finest jazz and supper club." Indeed, its reputation is deserved, for its Cajun-infused fare and performances by legends like Eartha Kitt and Mary Wilson. *1073 Wisconsin Ave. NW (at M St.). ☎ 202/337-4141. www. bluesalley.com. Cover $16–$75,*

Alternative acts drawn crowds at Black Cat.

plus $12 food and drink minimum, plus $4.50 surcharge. Metro: Foggy Bottom then Georgetown Metro Connection Shuttle.

★★ **Bohemian Caverns** U STREET CORRIDOR Calling itself the "sole home of soul jazz," this legendary joint has attracted A-list artists (Duke Ellington and Miles Davis among them) for decades. Its keyboard awning greets you, and its creative cavelike interior is like no other. *2001 11th St. NW (at U St.).* ☎ *202/299-0801. www. bohemiancaverns.com. Ticket prices vary. Entrees $9–$18. Metro: U St./ Cardozo*

★ **9:30 Club** U STREET CORRI-DOR Fans of '80s warblers Bob Mould and 'Ments frontman Paul Westerberg will love this intimate den for independent music. The best acoustic and lo-fi sets on the East Coast. *815 V St. NW (at Vermont Ave.).* ☎ *202/265-0930. www.930.com. Tickets $10–$50 in advance. Metro: U St./Cardozo*

Outdoor/Rooftop

★★ **International Bar** DOWN-TOWN Come for the classic cocktails in the lobby bar of the Washington Plaza Hotel, and then move outdoors to the poolside terrace and lounge, one of the only outdoor pool scenes in the D.C.

area. *10 Thomas Circle NW (at M St.).* ☎ *202/842-1300. www.washington plazahotel.com. Metro: McPherson Square.*

Local 16 U STREET CORRIDOR You might feel you're at a crowded house party in this renovated town-house turned bar that also happens to have one of the best rooftops for happy-hour mingling, dining, and drinking. *1602 U St. NW.* ☎ *202/ 265-2828. www.localsixteen.com. Metro: U St./Cardozo.*

★ **POV Bar** DOWNTOWN Order a martini and take in the view of the Washington Monument, the National Mall, and glimpses of the White House from this swanky bar in the W Hotel. *515 15th St. NW.* ☎ *202/661-2400. www.washington dc.com/povroofterrace. Metro: Metro Center*

Political Intrigue

★ **701** DOWNTOWN This posh restaurant between the White House and U.S. Capitol building attracts D.C.'s powerful movers and shakers. *701 Pennsylvania Ave. NW. 202/393-0701. www.701restaurant. com. Metro: Archives/Navy Memorial*

★ **Capital Grille Lounge** DOWNTOWN The premier political watering hole in town, this clubby lounge is witness to power-brokering, scandals, and plenty of

Appreciative crowds groove to lo-fi and acoustic sets at 9:30 Club.

cigar-tinged intrigue, all fueled by premium whiskeys and a wine list of some 300 bottles. *601 Pennsylvania Ave. NW (at 6th St.).* ☎ *202/737-6200. www.thecapitalgrille.com. Metro: Archives/Navy Memorial.*

★ Charlie Palmer Steak

DOWNTOWN   The city's elegant outpost for this nationally acclaimed chef attracts the town's top political dogs for stiff drinks and perfectly prepared sirloins. *101 Constitution Ave. NW (at Louisiana Ave.).* ☎ *202/547-8100. www.charlie palmer.com. Metro: Union Station.*

★ Martin's Tavern GEORGE-

TOWN   Chris Matthews, Tucker Carlson, and every president since Harry Truman have come to this "Old Washington" pub. Sidle up to the mahogany bar for a Scotch or take a seat in one of its booths, like the one where JFK proposed to Jackie. *1264 Wisconsin Ave. NW.* ☎ *202/333-7370. www.martins-tavern.com. No Metro access (see box, p 91).*

★★★ Round Robin Bar.

DOWNTOWN   Members of D.C.'s political elite have met in this centuries-old lounge in the Willard Intercontinental Hotel since the days of Abraham Lincoln. Order a classic mint julep and take in the drawings of its most famous historical patrons lining the green velvet walls. *1401 Pennsylvania Ave. NW. 202/628-9100. http://washington. intercontinental.com/food-drink/ round-robin-scotch-bar. Metro: Metro Center.*

★★ Off the Record Bar

DOWNTOWN   Billed as "Washington's place to be seen and not heard," Off the Record is just steps from the White House. I wish its red-paneled walls could talk. *In the Hay-Adams Hotel: 800 16th St. NW (at H St.).* ☎ *202/638-6600. www.hay adams.com. Metro: McPherson Sq.*

★ Tune Inn CAPITOL HILL   A

great happy hour and an eclectic dive bar vibe attract the just-out-of-college-and-working-on-the-Hill set, who down boozy beverages as they diss their famous bosses. *331 Pennsylvania Ave. SE.* ☎ *202/543-2725. Metro: Union Station*

Sports

★★ Green Turtle PENN QUAR-

TER   Basketball and hockey fans, this is your hotspot for catching the game on big-screen TVs, as well as all major sporting events, from Wimbledon to the Super Bowl. *601 F St. NW. 202/637-8889. www. thegreenturtle.com. Metro: Gallery Place/Chinatown.*

VIP Scene

★ Café Milano GEORGE-

TOWN   Rub shoulders with Botoxed socialites, back-slapping senators, and European playboys at the lively bar scene, or sit down for a meal of middling-to-good Italian fare. *3251 Prospect St. NW (at Potomac).* ☎ *202/333-6183. www. cafemilano.com. Metro: Foggy Bot-tom or Roslyn.*

Eighteenth Street Lounge

DUPONT CIRCLE   Some would say this multilevel meeting place has seen its heyday. But crowds of beautiful people still make their way through its unmarked front door to mingle on salon-style sofas and groove to live music. *1212 18th St. NW (at Connecticut Ave.).* ☎ *202/466-3922. Cover: $5–$20 Tues–Sat. Metro: Farragut North.*

★ The Park at 14th DOWN-

TOWN   Come dressed to kill for this velvet-roped multilevel lounge that attracts Hollywood starlets, famous athletes, and limo-riding fashionistas to its pulsing music, chic digs, and Dale Chihuly–esque chandeliers. *920 14th St. NW.*

National Harbor

If you're willing to make a day (or night of it), hop a cab or water taxi to **National Harbor,** just a few miles from downtown D.C. Here, you'll find shops along the waterfront, more than 30 restaurants, a carousel, and The Capital Wheel, a soaring 180-foot-tall Ferris wheel. The immense Gaylord National Resort Hotel stands out, and features an acclaimed steak restaurant, more stores, and a Bellagio-type fountain that shoots 60-feet (18m) in the air. Visitors can also rent paddleboards and kayaks here, and head out onto the Potomac. Call ☎ 877/628-5427 or visit www.nationalharbor. com for details.

☎ 202/737-7275. www.theparkat fourteenth.com. No cover. Metro: McPherson Square.

★★ U Street Music Hall. U
STREET CORRIDOR   This hopping basement dance club and live music venue is regularly packed with young people getting their groove on. 1115 U St. NW. 202/588-1889. www.ustreetmusichall.com. Metro: U St./Cardozo.

Whiskey Lovers
★★ Barrel CAPITOL HILL
"Brown water" takes center stage at this southern-inspired bar with nearly 100 varieties of bourbon, Scotch and whiskey on the menu. Small-batch cocktails and other elixirs are also available, along with a full food menu. 613 Pennsylvania Ave. SE. 202/543-3622. www.barrel dc.com. Metro: Eastern Market.

★★ Bourbon ADAMS MORGAN
Named for the 50 Kentucky bourbons (and assorted Tennessee varieties) poured here, this casual, modern pub attracts sports fans, slumming hipsters, grad students— even neighborhood families, who dine upstairs on tasty burgers and tater tots. 2321 18th St. NW ☎ 202/

332-0800. www.bourbondc.com. Metro: Dupont Circle or Woodley Park.

Wine Lovers
★★ Proof PENN QUARTER
More than 1,000 different bottles, some from the owner's own collection, and an Enomatic wine system that dispenses perfect pours by the glass make this trendy spot a must-taste for oenophiles. 775 G St. NW. ☎ 202/737-7663. www.proofdc. com. Metro: Gallery Place/ Chinatown.

★★★ 1789 GEORGETOWN
This low-lit, classic New American restaurant has a romantic bar, a fireplace, and one of the city's most impressive wine lists. 1226 36th St. NW (at Prospect St.). ☎ 202/965-1789. www.1789restaurant.com. No Metro access (see box, p 91).

★★ Sonoma CAPITOL HILL   The
hot spot on the Hill, serving American small plates with more than 35 well-chosen wines by the glass or bottle. Be prepared to get friendly with strangers; the place is always packed and tables are thisclose. 223 Pennsylvania Ave. SE (at 2nd St.). ☎ 202/544-8088. www.sonomadc. com. Metro: Capitol South. ●

D.C. **Arts & Entertainment**

Rock Creek

EMBASSY ROW

Kalorama Rd. NW

Columbia Rd. NW

Florida Ave. NW

California St. NW

Massachusetts

S St. NW

Connecticut Ave. NW

19th St.

18th St.

NW

T St. NW

V St. NW

U St. NW

16th St. NW

15th St. NW

14th St. NW

OAK HILL CEMETERY

ROCK CREEK PARK

Sheridan Circle

Florida Ave.

Dupont Circle NW

S St. NW

R St. NW

Q St. NW

29th St. NW

28th St. NW

Rock Cr. Pkwy.

Q St. NW

P St. NW

Dupont Circle M

P St. NW

7

Q St. NW

6

GEORGETOWN

O St. NW

ROCK CREEK PARK

Massachusetts

P St. NW

Scott Circle

Rhode Island

Vermont

N St. NW

N St. NW

Ave. NW

DUPONT CIRCLE

N St.

M St. NW

Thomas Circle

22nd St.

21st St. NW

20th St. NW

19th St. NW

New Hampshire

M St. NW

L St.

NW

Pennsylvania

1

29

Washington Circle

K St. NW

Farragut North M

5

Farragut Square

Farragut

McPherson Square

29

17th St.

16th St.

15th St.

14th St.

I St. NW

I St. NW

Rock Creek and Potomac Pkwy. NW

Foggy Bottom-GWU M

GEORGE WASHINGTON UNIVERSITY

Farragut West M

H St. NW

McPherson Square M

Watergate

66

H St. NW

18th St.

Lafayette Square

Pennsylvania Ave. NW

G St. NW

G St. NW

FOGGY BOTTOM

F St. NW

Kennedy Center

2

E St. Expwy.

E St. NW

E St. NW

White House

15th St.

14th St.

Freedom

23rd St.

Virginia Ave. NW

3

17th St.

66

C St. NW

The Ellipse

1 50

Theodore Roosevelt Memorial Bridge

Constitution Ave. NW

Constitution Gardens Lake

Lincoln Memorial

Vietnam Veterans Memorial

Constitution Gardens

Reflecting Pool

Washington Monument

Arlington Memorial Bridge

Korean War Veterans Memorial

50

Independence Ave. SW

Independence Ave. SW

Independence Ave. SW

14th St. SW

Martin Luther King, Jr. Memorial

WEST POTOMAC PARK

Cherry Trees

Maine Ave.

LADY BIRD JOHNSON PARK

Potomac

FDR Memorial

Tidal Basin

Cherry Trees

1 SW

VIRGINIA

River

Ohio Dr. SW

Jefferson Memorial

Washington Blvd.

George Mason Memorial

395

Previous page: Fireworks over Wolf Trap theater in Virginia.

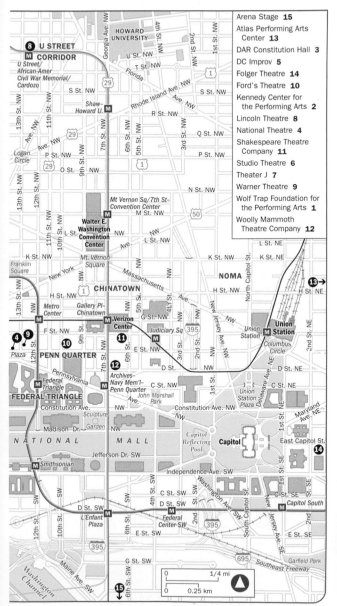

Arena Stage **15**
Atlas Performing Arts Center **13**
DAR Constitution Hall **3**
DC Improv **5**
Folger Theatre **14**
Ford's Theatre **10**
Kennedy Center for the Performing Arts **2**
Lincoln Theatre **8**
National Theatre **4**
Shakespeare Theatre Company **11**
Studio Theatre **6**
Theater J **7**
Warner Theatre **9**
Wolf Trap Foundation for the Performing Arts **1**
Woolly Mammoth Theatre Company **12**

Arts & Entertainment Best Bets

Ford's Theater.

Best **Restored Theater**
★ The Lincoln Theatre, *1215 U St. NW* (p 158)

Best for **History Buffs**
★★ Ford's Theatre, *511 10th St. NW* (p 157)

Best for **High-Brow Performance**
★★★ Kennedy Center for the Performing Arts, *2700 F St. NW* (p 158)

Best for **Avant-Garde Acts**
★★ Woolly Mammoth Theatre Company, *641 D St. NW* (p 158)

Best Place to **Laugh So Hard You Cry**
★★ DC Improv, *1140 Connecticut Ave. NW* (p 157)

Best of the **Bard**
★★ Shakespeare Theatre Company, *610 F St. NW* (p 158)

Best for **Touring Broadway Shows**
★★ National Theatre, *1321 Pennsylvania Ave. NW* (p 158)

Best for **Edgy Playwrights**
★★ Studio Theatre, *1501 14th St. NW* (p 158)

Best **Outdoor Theater**
★ Wolf Trap Foundation for the Performing Arts, *1645 Trap Rd., Vienna, Virginia* (p 158)

You can picnic on the lawn while enjoying a show at Wolf Trap.

Arts & Entertainment A to Z

The Arena Stage entrance at The Mead Center for American Theater.

★★ **Arena Stage** SW WATERFRONT   Artistic Director Molly Smith is known for staging first-rate classical and contemporary productions, attracting leading men and women from New York and Hollywood. *1101 6th St. SW (at Maine Ave.).* ☎ *202/488-3300. www.arenastage.org. Ticket prices vary. Metro: Waterfront–SEU.*

★ **Atlas Performing Arts Center** H STREET   A cornerstone of the revitalized H Street corridor, this venue combines community installations with larger-scale festivals and events like Step Afrika! and jazz and dance performances. *1333 H St. NE. Box Office:* ☎ *202/399-7993 ext. 2. www.atlasarts.org. Ticket prices vary. Metro: Union Station.*

★★★ **DAR Constitution Hall** DOWNTOWN   Everyone from Aretha Franklin to the Smashing Pumpkins has played this popular venue for household-name musicians, comedians, and lecturers. *17th Street between C and D sts., NW.* ☎ *202/628-1776. www.dar.*

org. *Ticket prices vary. Metro: Farragut West or Farragut North.*

★★ **DC Improv** DOWNTOWN   Before they hit big, Ellen DeGeneres and Dave Chappelle performed at this underground comedy club that still draws top-notch artists weekly from across the country. *1140 Connecticut Ave. NW.* ☎ *202/296-7008. www.dcimprov.com. Tickets are $15–$20. Metro: Farragut North.*

★★ **Folger Theatre** CAPITOL HILL   Buy tickets here for Shakespearean plays, concerts, and literary readings, as well as fun family activities with a historical twist. *201 E. Capitol St. SE (between 2nd and 3rd sts.).* ☎ *202/544-7077. www.folger.edu. Tickets $25–$49. Metro: Capitol South.*

★★ **Ford's Theatre** DOWNTOWN   This theater, where President Lincoln was shot in 1865 while watching the comedy *Our American Cousin*, is still staging compelling productions today. *511 10th St. NW (between E and F sts.).* ☎ *202/347-4833. www.fordstheatre.org. Ticket prices vary. Metro: Metro Center.*

Performance at the DAR Constitution Hall.

★★★ Kennedy Center for the Performing Arts FOGGY BOTTOM Named for the late president, this Washington landmark is both a living memorial and a first-class venue for symphonies, operas, ballets, and touring theatrical and dance productions—not to mention their annual awards. *2700 F St. NW (between New Hampshire Ave. and Rock Creek Pkwy.). Tours ☎ 202/416-8340; box office ☎ 202/467-4600. www.kennedy-center.org. Tickets $14–$290. Metro: Foggy Bottom.*

★ The Lincoln Theatre U STREET CORRIDOR Restored to its original splendor, this historic venue has welcomed a host of African-American musicians, from Duke Ellington and Billie Holliday to modern entertainers such as Dick Gregory. *1215 U St. NW (between 12th and 13th sts.). ☎ 877/987-6487. www.thelincolndc.com. Tickets $20–$200. Metro: U St./Cardozo*

★★ National Theatre DOWNTOWN Everyone from Dame Edna to Earth, Wind & Fire plays this historic "theater of Presidents," open since 1835. *1321 Pennsylvania Ave., NW (between 13th and 14th sts.). ☎ 202/628-6161. www.thenationaldc.org. Tickets $37–$86. Metro: Metro Center or Federal Triangle.*

★★ Shakespeare Theatre Company PENN QUARTER Catch the Bard's best, from *A Midsummer Night's Dream* to *Othello*, in productions with astounding sets and nationally known actors. *610 F St. NW (between 6th and 7th sts.). ☎ 202/547-1122. www.shakespearetheatre.org. Tickets $23–$68. Metro: Gallery Place/Chinatown or Judiciary Square.*

★★ Studio Theatre 14TH STREET This theater has earned a stellar reputation for edgy, contemporary productions by playwrights such as Neil LaBute. Its newly renovated space is the crown jewel of the recently revived 14th Street/Logan Circle area. *1501 14th St. NW (at P St.). ☎ 202/332-3300. www.studiotheatre.org. Tickets $32–$62. Metro: U St./Cardozo, Dupont Circle, or McPherson Square.*

★ Theater J DOWNTOWN This company is nationally and internationally renowned for its progressive Jewish theater programs. *1529 16th St. NW. ☎ 202/518-9400. www.washingtondcjcc.org. Tickets $15–$45. Metro: Dupont Circle.*

★★ Warner Theatre CAPITOL HILL This big theater stages a range of performances, from international recording artists (Bob Weir, Hall & Oates) to touring plays (*Golda's Balcony*, *Cheaters*), to comedic one-man shows (Lewis Black, William Shatner). *513 13th St. NW (between E and F sts.). ☎ 202/783-4000. www.warnertheatre.com. Ticket prices vary. Metro: Metro Center.*

★ Wolf Trap Foundation for the Performing Arts NORTHERN VIRGINIA Year-round, enjoy touring pop, country, folk, and blues artists, plus dance, theater, opera, and orchestra performances—with outdoor plays and concerts in summer. *1645 Trap Rd. (off Rte. 7), Vienna, Virginia. ☎ 877/WOLF-TRAP [965-3872]. www.wolftrap.org. Tickets $10–$70. No Metro access.*

★★ Woolly Mammoth Theatre Company PENN QUARTER This provocative, experimental company aims to break new ground, showcasing original works by emerging artists. Provocative, experimental, never boring. *641 D St. NW (at 7th St.). ☎ 202/289-2443. www.woollymammoth.net. Tickets $22–$52. Metro: Archives/Navy Memorial or Gallery Place/Chinatown.* ●

D.C. Hotels

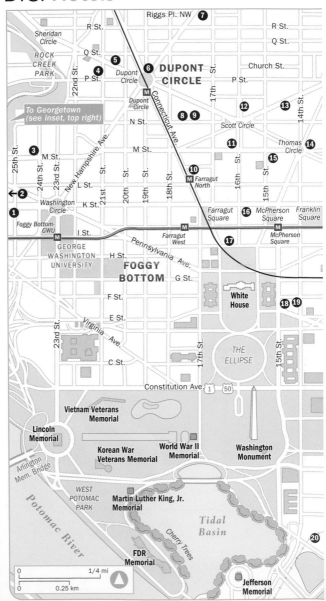

Previous page: Federal Suite of the Hay Adams

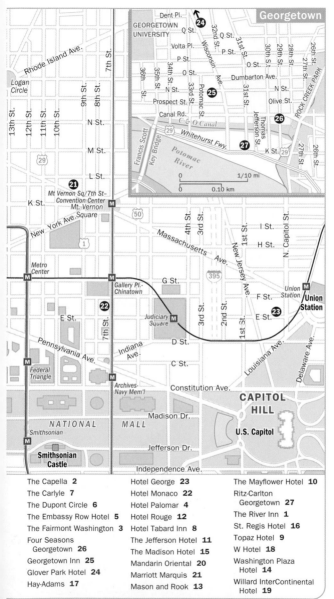

Georgetown

The Capella **2**

The Carlyle **7**

The Dupont Circle **6**

The Embassy Row Hotel **5**

The Fairmont Washington **3**

Four Seasons
  Georgetown **26**

Georgetown Inn **25**

Glover Park Hotel **24**

Hay-Adams **17**

Hotel George **23**

Hotel Monaco **22**

Hotel Palomar **4**

Hotel Rouge **12**

Hotel Tabard Inn **8**

The Jefferson Hotel **11**

The Madison Hotel **15**

Mandarin Oriental **20**

Marriott Marquis **21**

Mason and Rook **13**

The Mayflower Hotel **10**

Ritz-Carlton
  Georgetown **27**

The River Inn **1**

St. Regis Hotel **16**

Topaz Hotel **9**

W Hotel **18**

Washington Plaza
  Hotel **14**

Willard InterContinental
  Hotel **19**

Hotel Best Bets

Where **Activist Hollywood A-Listers Hold Court**
★★ Mandarin Oriental $$$ *1330 Maryland Ave. SW (p 166)*

Where **Hollywood A-Listers Get Some Sleep**
★★ Gold Floor at The Fairmont Washington $$$ *2401 M St. NW (p 163)*

Where Washington's **Young Bucks Mingle**
★★ Hotel George $$ *15 E St. NW (p 165)*

Most Romantic **Bathtub with the Best View**
★★ Willard InterContinental $$$ *1401 Pennsylvania Ave. NW (p 168)*

For Some **Shabby with Your Chic**
★★ Tabard Inn $$ *1739 N St. NW (p 165)*

Where to **Make a Great Splash**
★★ Washington Plaza (and its rooftop pool) $$ *10 Thomas Circle NW (p 168)*

Best for **Fashionistas**
★★★ Four Seasons Georgetown $$$$ *2800 Pennsylvania Ave. NW (p 164)*

Best for **Warehouse Luxe**
★★★ Ritz-Carlton Georgetown $$$$ *3100 S St. NW (p 167)*

Where to Meet an **NBA Player**
★★ Hotel Monaco $$ *700 F St. NW (p 165)*

Best for the **Entitled**
★★ The Madison Hotel $$$ *1177 15th St. NW (p 166)*

Best for **History Buffs**
★★★ Hay-Adams $$$ *800 16th St. NW. (p 164)*

Best for **Astrology Fanatics**
★★ Topaz Hotel $$$ *733 N St. NW (p 167)*

Best for **Fans of All Things Red**
★★ Hotel Rouge $$ *1315 16th St. NW (p 165)*

Best for **Conference Goers**
★ Marriott Marquis $$ *901 Massachusetts Ave. NW. (p 166)*

The Capella Hotel on the Georgetown C&O Canal.

Hotels A to Z

Guest room at the Carlyle Hotel.

★★★ **The Capella** GEORGE-TOWN   Well-heeled travelers will find luxurious rooms with views of Georgetown's C&O Canal, along with a private rooftop deck and the signature Rye Bar featuring a variety of whiskeys and other cocktails. *1050 31st St. NW.* ☎ *202/617-2400. www.capellahotels.com/washington dc/georgetown. 39 units. Doubles from $600. AE, MC, V. No Metro access.*

★★ **The Carlyle.** DUPONT CIRCLE Walk to Dupont Circle, the White House and many other D.C. attractions from this revamped Art Deco hotel, which features cozy Tempur-Pedic mattresses, flatscreen TVs, and full service kitchens (available in some rooms). *1731 New Hampshire Ave. NW.* ☎ *877/301-0019 or 202/234-3200. www.carlylehoteldc. com. 198 units. Doubles from $289. AE, MC, V. Metro: Dupont Circle*

★★★ **The Dupont Circle** DUPONT CIRCLE   This modern, comfortable hotel is centrally located (many rooms even overlook Dupont Circle), and offers free Wi-Fi access and an upscale restaurant. Stay on Level 9 and you'll have exclusive access to a private elevator and lounge. *1500 New Hampshire Ave. NW* ☎ *202/483-6000. www.dupontatthecircle.com. 327 units. Doubles from $119. AE, DISC, MC, V. Metro: Dupont Circle.*

The Embassy Row Hotel DUPONT CIRCLE   Recently refurbished rooms and a two-level rooftop bar with a pool woo patrons to this stylish hotel, just steps from Dupont Circle. Its "adult playground" features ping-pong and foosball tables for guests. *2015 Massachusetts Ave. NW.* ☎ *855/893-1011 or 202/265-1600. www.destinationhotels.com/embassy-row-hotel. 231 units. Doubles from $179. Metro: Dupont Circle.*

★★ **The Fairmont Washington** WEST END   Lush atrium gardens set the tone for this elegant, clubby, luxury hotel. Its Gold Floor

Double room at the Fairmont.

caters to A-listers with free car service, chocolates, and even a pillow
menu. *2401 M St. NW (at 24th St.
NW).* ☎ *866/540-4505 or 202/429-
2400. www.fairmont.com/washington.
415 units. Doubles from $279. AE,
DISC, MC, V. Metro: Foggy Bottom
or Dupont Circle.*

★★★ Four Seasons George-
town GEORGETOWN   Travel editors, fashionistas, and movie stars in
town to film political thrillers book
here for the unparalleled quality
and service. The lower-level spa is
the capital's best, and M Street
shopping is steps away. *2800 Pennsylvania Ave. NW (at M St. NW).*
☎ *202/342-0444. www.fourseasons.
com/washington. 211 units. Doubles*

The Spa at the Four Seasons Georgetown.

*from $299. AE, DC, DISC, MC, V.
Metro: Foggy Bottom.*

kids Georgetown Inn GEORGE-
TOWN   If you want to be in the
heart of Georgetown, this decent (if
unspectacular) hotel is the place to
stay. Its clubby, dark-wooded interior underwent renovations in 2011,
and the Daily Grill downstairs is
family-friendly. *1310 Wisconsin Ave.
NW (at N St. NW).* ☎ *866/344-8750.
www.georgetowninn.com. 96 units.
Doubles $195–$245. AE, DC, DISC,
MC, V. No Metro access. Bus: 30, 32,
or 34.*

Glover Park Hotel GLOVER
PARK   Perched high above Wisconsin Avenue in the residential
neighborhood of Glover Park, this
newly opened hotel features urban
design in its brick walls and wood-
and-steel finishes, along with luxe
and comfortable guestrooms. *2505
Wisconsin Ave. NW.* ☎ *202/337-
9700. www.gloverparkhotel.com. 154
units. Doubles from $269. AE, DC,
DISC, MC, V. No Metro access.*

★★★ Hay-Adams DOWN-
TOWN   Steps from the White
House, this luxury hotel has great
views of Lafayette Park and oozes
European elegance. It's also home
to Off the Record Bar, a buzzy
haunt for D.C. insiders. *800 16th St.*

NW. ☎ 202/638-6600. www.hay
adams.com. 145 units. Doubles from
$299. AE, DC, DISC, MC, V. Metro:
Farragut West or McPherson Square.

★★ **Hotel George** CAPITOL
HILL   Modern, minimalist, chic. Hill
staffers flock to the hotel bar, at
Bistro Bis, and the first president
himself welcomes travelers to the
capital in the silkscreen dollar-bill
prints that hang in every guest
room. 15 E St. NW (at N. Capitol
NW). ☎ 800/576-8331 or 202/347-
4200. www.hotelgeorge.com. 139
units. Doubles from $409. AE, DC,
DISC, MC, V. Metro: Capitol Hill.

★★ **Hotel Monaco** PENN
QUARTER   Housed in a landmark
former post office, this temple to
modern cool juxtaposes historic
marble and sky-high ceilings with
sleek, inviting guest rooms. Poste,
the swank bar downstairs, attracts
visiting NBA stars (from the Verizon
Center down the block), who
"hoop" it up in style. 700 F St. NW
(at 7th St. NW). ☎ 877/649-1202 or
202/628-7177. www.monaco-dc.com.
84 units. Doubles from $429. AE, DC,
DISC, MC, V. Metro: Gallery Place/
Chinatown.

★★ **Hotel Palomar** DUPONT
CIRCLE   Art takes center stage at
this luxury hotel, which offers

comfortably appointed rooms with
crisp Frette linens and faux lynx
throws, plus a stylish restaurant. Pet
friendly, too. 2121 P St. NW.
☎ 877/866-3070 or 202/448-1800.
www.hotelpalomar-dc.com. 335 units.
Doubles from $389. Metro: Dupont
Circle.

★★ **Hotel Rouge** DUPONT
CIRCLE   Young renegades who are
into high-tech hotels will love the
red-hot accommodations at this
racy inn. Specialty rooms feature
flat-panel computer monitors, HD
TVs, Xboxes, and video game
libraries. 1315 16th St. NW (between
Massachusetts Ave. and Scott Circle).
☎ 202/232-8000. www.rougehotel.
com. 137 units. Doubles from $339.
AE, DC, DISC, MC, V. Metro: Dupont
Circle.

★★ **The Tabard Inn** DUPONT
CIRCLE   Every room in this eclectic
inn is a romantic mix of original art
and fine early-20th-century
antiques. The excellent restaurant
has a lovely summer garden, cozy
divans, and a fireplace for cold
nights. Some rooms have shared
baths. 1739 N St. NW (between 17th
and 18th sts.). ☎ 202/785-1277.
www.tabardinn.com. 40 units. Doubles with private bathroom from
$240. AE, DC, DISC, MC, V. Metro:
Dupont Circle or Farragut North.

Guestroom at Glover Park.

The Hotel Monaco is set in a former post office.

★★ The Jefferson Hotel.

DOWNTOWN Built in 1923, this stately hotel is just four blocks from the White House. Dine out at its award-winning restaurant, Plume, then retire for a nightcap in the library or in the cozy lounge, Quill. *1200b 16th St. NW. 202/448-2300. www.jeffersondc.com. 99 units. Doubles from $550. Metro: Farragut North or Farragut West*

★★ The Madison Hotel

DOWNTOWN Famed for fawning over foreign dignitaries, The Madison is exactly how you'd imagine a small Washington hotel to be: traditional, quiet, well kept, and, yes, dignified. Spice things up by dining or drinking at trendy Rural Society downstairs. *1177 15th St. NW (at M St. NW). 800/424-8577 or 202/862-1600. www.loewshotels.com. 356 units. Doubles from $229. AE, DC, DISC, MC, V. Metro: Farragut North.*

★★ Mandarin Oriental

SOUTHWEST A feng shui expert designed the rooms here—some with spectacular views of the Southwest Marina and the Jefferson Memorial. Eastern meets Western luxury in the beautifully balanced silk wall coverings, bamboo embellishments, and marble bathrooms. *1330 Maryland Ave. SW (at 12th St. SW). 888/888-1778 or 202/554-8588. www.mandarinoriental.com/washington. 400 units. Doubles from $255. AE, DC, DISC, MC, V. Metro: Smithsonian.*

★ Marriott Marquis

DOWNTOWN In town for a convention? Or just want to stay in the heart of it all? This massive hotel is connected to the Convention Center, adjacent to the new downtown City Center, and just a few blocks from Penn Quarter. Stay on site and shop at the many stores on its ground floor. *901 Massachusetts Ave. NW. 202/824-9200. www.marriott.com. 1,224 units. Doubles from $239. Metro: Gallery Place/Chinatown or McPherson Square.*

Mason and Rook

DOWNTOWN It's like staying at a friend's coveted urban apartment at this Logan Circle hotel. Large guestrooms, spacious marble bathrooms, and an indoor/outdoor lounge and bar are just some of the features here. *1430 Rhode Island Avenue, NW. 202/742-3100. www.masonandrookhotel.com. 178 units. Doubles from $409. Metro: Farragut North*

★★ The Mayflower Hotel

DOWNTOWN The quintessential grande dame of Washington, this historic hotel with a marble interior lobby and well-appointed rooms is still comfortable enough to make you feel right at home. *1127 Connecticut Ave. NW.* ☎ *202/347-3000. 583 units and 74 suites. Doubles from $250. AE, DISC, MC, V. Metro: Farragut North.*

★★★ Ritz-Carlton Georgetown

GEORGETOWN Historic architecture meets modern elegance in this upscale hotel, once the site of a 19th-century brick-and-steel incinerator. If the guest rooms' marble bathrooms and goose-down pillows don't soothe your soul, book a treatment at the pampering spa. *3100 South St. NW (at 31st St. NW).* ☎ *800/241-3333 or 202/912-4100. www.ritzcarlton.com/hotels/georgetown. 86 units. Doubles from $349. AE, DC, DISC, MC, V. No Metro access (see box, p 91).*

★ kids The River Inn

FOGGY BOTTOM If you love to travel but hate to blow all your cash dining out, book at this centrally located, all-suite hotel; each spacious guestroom has a full kitchenette. *924 25th St. NW (at K St. NW).* ☎ *202/*

Some rooms at the posh Mandarin Oriental Hotel have water views.

337-7600. www.theriverinn.com. 126 units. Doubles from $99. AE, DC, DISC, MC, V. Metro: Foggy Bottom.

★★★ St. Regis Hotel

DOWNTOWN This stately hotel a mere few blocks from the White House was restored to its original 1926 glamour, featuring luxurious rooms in tranquil tones and a relaxing spa. *923 16th and K sts. NW.* ☎ *202/638-2626. www.stregiswashingtondc.com. 179 units. Doubles from $190–$460. Metro: Farragut North.*

★★ Topaz Hotel

DUPONT CIRCLE This funky boutique hotel offers complimentary bikes and yoga equipment, plus exotic interior textures and healing in-room

Guest rooms at the Ritz Carlton have luxe touches such as marble bathrooms.

One of Mason and Rook's spacious guestrooms.

spa services. *1733 N St. NW (between 17th and 18th sts.).* ☎ *202/393-3000. www.topazhotel. com. 99 units. Doubles from $349. AE, DC, DISC, MC, V. Metro: Dupont Circle or Farragut North.*

★ **W Hotel** DOWNTOWN   Just blocks from the White House and National Mall, this swank hotel offers all of the modern and efficient services you'll need with a prime location in the center of D.C. Its POV rooftop bar offers spectacular views of the city below. *515 15th St. NW.* ☎ *202/661-2400. www.wwashingtondc.com. 317 units. Doubles from $329. AE, DISC, MC, V. Metro: Metro Center*

★★ **Washington Plaza Hotel** LOGAN CIRCLE   Rich and famous hipsters who might otherwise be in Miami flock here for the exclusive

outdoor pool and buzzing scene at the International Bar. *10 Thomas Circle NW (at 14th St. NW).* ☎ *800/ 424-1140 or 202/842-1300. www. washingtonplazahotel.com. 340 units. Doubles from $189. AE, DC, DISC, MC, V. Metro: McPherson Square.*

★★ **Willard InterContinental Hotel** DOWNTOWN   Beaux-Arts architecture meets history here— where Martin Luther King, Jr., wrote his "I Have a Dream" speech, and nearly every president since Grant has bunked at least once for the night. Ask about the romantic tub in the honeymoon suite. *1401 Pennsylvania Ave. NW (at 14th St. NW).* ☎ *800/827-1747 or 202/628-9100. www.washington.intercontinental. com. 341 units. Doubles from $239. AE, DC, DISC, MC, V. Metro: Metro Center.* ●

The
Savvy Traveler

Before You Go

Government Tourist Offices

Destination D.C., 901 7th St. NW, 4th Floor, Washington, DC 20001-3719 (☎ **800/422-8644** or 202/789-7000; www.washington.org) provides information on hotels, restaurants, sights, shops, and more.

Also take a look at the D.C. government's website, **www.dc.gov**, and Cultural Tourism D.C., **www.culturaltourismdc.org**, for more information about the city.

For additional information about Washington's most popular tourist spots, access the National Park Service website, **www.nps.gov/nacc** and the Smithsonian Institution's **www.si.edu**.

The Best Times to Go

The city's peak seasons generally coincide with the sessions of Congress and springtime. When Congress is "in," from about the second week in September until Thanksgiving, and again from about mid-January through June, hotels are full with guests on business.

Mid-March through June traditionally is the most frenzied season, when families and school groups descend to see the cherry blossoms. It's also a popular season for protest marches.

To avoid crowds, consider visiting at the end of August and early September or between Thanksgiving and mid-January—though the lighting of the National Christmas Tree is very popular.

The July 4th Independence Day celebration is spectacular, but the weather is very hot and humid in July and August. Many of Washington's performance stages close, although some outdoor arenas and parks host events.

For event schedules, see **www.washington.org, www.culturaltourismdc.org, www.dc.gov**, and **www.washingtonpost.com**.

Useful Numbers & Websites

- **National Park Service** (☎ **202/426-6841;** www.nps.gov/state/dc). You reach a real person and not a recording when you phone this number with questions about the monuments, The Mall, national park lands, and events taking place at these locations.

- The **Washington, D.C., Visitor Information Center** (☎ 202/312-1300; www.itcdc.com) is a small visitors center in the immense Ronald Reagan International Trade Center Building (1300 Pennsylvania Ave. NW).

- The **Smithsonian Information Center,** in the "Castle," 1000 Jefferson Dr. SW (☎ **202/633-1000**; www.si.edu), is open every day but Christmas from 8:30am to 5:30pm.

- The **American Automobile Association (AAA)** has a large central office near the White House, at 1405 G St. NW, between G Street and New York Avenue NW, Washington, DC 20005-2111 (☎ **202/481-6811**).

Ronald Reagan International Airport.

AVERAGE TEMPERATURE & RAINFALL IN WASHINGTON, D.C.

	JAN	FEB	MAR	APR	MAY	JUNE
Avg. High (°F/ °C)	44/5	46/8	4/12	66/19	76/25	83/29
Avg. Low (°F/°C)	30/-1	29/-1	36/2	46/8	54/14	65/19
Rainfall (in.)	3.21	2.63	3.6	2.71	3.82	3.13

	JULY	AUG	SEPT	OCT	NOV	DEC
Avg. High (°F/ °C)	87/31	85/30	79/26	68/20	57/14	46/8
Avg. Low (°F/°C)	69/20	68/20	61/16	50/15	39/4	32/0
Rainfall (in.)	3.66	3.44	3.79	3.22	3.03	3.05

Getting **There**

By Plane

Domestic airlines with scheduled flights into all three of Washington, D.C.'s, airports, Washington Dulles International **(Dulles)**, Ronald Reagan Washington National **(National)**, and Baltimore–Washington International **(BWI)**, include **American** (☎ 800/433-7300; www.aa.com), **Delta** (☎ 800/221-1212; www.delta.com), and **United** (☎ 800/864-8331; www.united.com).

Quite a few low-fare airlines serve all three D.C. airports. **Southwest Airlines** (☎ 800/435-9792; www.southwest.com), at **BWI Airport,** has more than 200 daily flights to more than 35 cities. Another bargain airline at BWI is **JetBlue** (☎ 800/538-2583; www.jetblue.com).

Discount airlines that serve **Dulles** are **Virgin Atlantic** (☎ 800/359-8474; www.virgin-atlantic.com), **Southwest, JetBlue** (☎ 800/538-2583; www.jetblue.com), and **Frontier** (☎ 800/432-1359; www.frontierairlines.com).

Two discount airlines use **National Airport: Frontier** (☎ 800/432-1359; www.frontierairlines.com) and **Virgin America** (☎ 877/359-8474; www.virginamerica.com).

Shuttle Service from New York, Boston & Chicago

Delta and American continue to dominate the D.C.–East Coast shuttle service. Between the two of them, hourly or almost-hourly shuttle service runs between Boston's Logan Airport and Washington, and New York's La Guardia Airport and Washington. The **Delta Shuttle** (☎ 800/221-1212) travels daily between New York and Washington, while the **American Airlines Shuttle** (☎ 800/433-7300) operates daily between Boston and Washington and New York and Washington. **Southwest** (see details above) offers nearly hourly service daily between BWI and Chicago's Midway Airport, Providence, Hartford, Long Island, Manchester (New Hampshire), Orlando, and Nashville.

Getting into Town from the Airport

The following transportation options are available at all three airports.

TAXI SERVICE For a trip downtown, expect a taxi to cost anywhere from $10 to $20 for the 10- to 15-minute ride from National Airport; $60 to $68 for the 30- to 40-minute ride from Dulles Airport; and $90 for the 45-minute ride from BWI.

SHUTTLES Vans (☎ 800/258-3826; www.supershuttle.com) offer shared-ride, door-to-door service, but be prepared for them to make other stops before reaching your destination. Book online or over the phone in advance, or at the airport when your plane lands. If you arrive after midnight, call the 24-hour toll-free number above. To reach downtown, expect to pay about $14, plus $10 for each additional person from National; $29, plus $10 per additional person from Dulles; and $25 for the shared van, plus $12 per additional person from BWI. If you're calling SuperShuttle for a ride from D.C. to an airport, reserve at least 24 hours in advance.

Free hotel/motel shuttles operate from all three airports to certain nearby properties. Ask about such transportation when you book a room at your hotel.

LUXURY SEDANS Prices vary significantly for ExecuCar private car transportation downtown. For pickup from BWI or IAD, reserve passage by calling ☎ 800/410-4444; for pickup from National, try **Red Select Cars** (☎ 703/777-7777) or consult the Yellow Pages.

Individual transportation options at each airport are as follows:

FROM RONALD REAGAN WASHINGTON NATIONAL AIRPORT Metrorail's (☎ 202/637-7000) Yellow and Blue lines stop at the airport and connect via an enclosed walkway to level two, the concourse level, of the main terminal, adjacent to terminals B and C. The ride downtown takes 15 to 20 minutes (longer at rush hour). It is safe, convenient, and cheap. The maximum fare to any station on the Metrorail system is less than $6 when using a SmarTrip card, available inside the Metro station.

Metrobuses (☎ 202/637-7000) also serve the area, should you be going somewhere off the Metro route, but Metrorail is faster.

If you're renting a car from on-site **car-rental** agencies **Alamo** (☎ 800/462-5266), **Avis** (☎ 800/331-1212), **Budget** (☎ 800/527-0700), **Enterprise** (☎ 800/736-8222), **Hertz** (☎ 800/654-3131), or **National** (☎ 800/227-7368), go to level two, the concourse level, follow the pedestrian walkway to the parking garage, find garage A, and descend one flight. You can also take the free Airport Shuttle (look for the sign on the curb outside the terminal) to parking garage A. If you've rented from off-premises agencies such as **Dollar** (☎ 800/800-4000), head outside the baggage claim area of your terminal, and catch the shuttle bus marked for your agency.

To get downtown by car, follow the signs for the George Washington Parkway. Then take I-395 North to Washington. Take the I-395 North exit, which takes you across the 14th Street Bridge. Stay in the left lane crossing the bridge and follow the signs for Route 1, which will put you on 14th Street NW. Ask your hotel for directions from 14th Street and Constitution Avenue NW.

A more scenic route runs to the left of the GW Parkway as you follow the signs for Memorial Bridge. You'll be driving alongside the Potomac River, with the monuments in view; then, as you cross over Memorial Bridge, the Lincoln Memorial greets you. Stay left coming over the bridge, swoop around left of the Memorial, turn left on 23rd Street NW, right on Constitution Avenue, and then left again on 15th Street NW (the Washington Monument will be to your right), into the heart of downtown.

FROM WASHINGTON DULLES INTERNATIONAL AIRPORT The

Washington Flyer Silver Line Express Bus runs between Dulles and the Wiehle-Reston East Metro station, where you can board a train for D.C. In the airport, purchase tickets at the counter located inside Arrivals Door #4 in the Main Terminal. Buses to the Wiehle-Reston East Metro station run daily, every 15 minutes during peak times and 20 minutes during off-peak times, and cost $5 one-way.

Also convenient is the **Metrobus** that runs between Dulles and the L'Enfant Plaza Metro station, within walking distance of the National Mall and Smithsonian museums. The bus departs hourly, costs only $7 with a SmarTrip, and takes 45 to 60 minutes.

For rental car pick-up at Dulles, head down the ramp near your baggage claim area, and walk outside to the curb to look for your rental car's shuttle bus stop. The buses come by every 5 minutes or so en route to nearby rental lots. These include **Alamo** (📞 888/826-6893), **Avis** (📞 703/661-3500), **Budget** (📞 703/437-9559), **Dollar** (📞 866/434-2226), **Enterprise** (📞 703/661-8800), **Hertz** (📞 703/471-6020), **National** (📞 877/222-9058), and **Thrifty** (📞 877/283-0898).

To reach downtown from Dulles by car, exit the airport and stay on the Dulles Access Road, which leads right into I-66 east. Follow I-66 east, which takes you across the Theodore Roosevelt Memorial Bridge; be sure to stay in the center lane as you cross the bridge, and this will put you on Constitution Avenue. Ask your hotel for directions from this point.

FROM BALTIMORE–WASHINGTON INTERNATIONAL AIRPORT Washington's Metro service runs an **Express Metro Bus** ("B30") between its Metrorail Green Line Greenbelt station and BWI Airport. In the airport,

head to the lower level and look for "Public Transit" signs to find the bus, which runs daily every 40 minutes, takes about 30 minutes, and costs $7. At the Greenbelt Metro station, you purchase a Metro fare card or SmarTrip card and board a Metro train, which will take you into the city. Depending on where you want to go, you can either stay on the Green Line train to your designated stop or get off at the Fort Totten Station to transfer to a Red Line train, whose stops include Union Station (near Capitol Hill) and various downtown locations.

Amtrak (📞 800/872-7245) and **Maryland Rural Commuter (MARC;** 📞 800/743-3682) trains also run into the city. Both travel between the BWI Railway Station (📞 410/672-6169) and Washington's Union Station (📞 202/289-1908), about a 30-minute ride. Amtrak's service is daily (ticket prices range $15–$38 per person, one-way, depending on time and train type), while MARC's is weekdays only ($7 per person, one-way). A courtesy shuttle runs every 10 minutes or so between the airport and the train station; stop at the desk near the baggage-claim area to check for train or bus departure times. Trains depart about every hour.

BWI operates a large, off-site, car-rental facility. From the ground transportation area, a shuttle bus transports you to the lot. Rental agencies include **Avis** (📞 410/859-1680), **Alamo** (📞 410/859-8092), **Budget** (📞 410/850-4437), **Dollar** (📞 410/850-7112), **Enterprise** (800/325-8007), **Hertz** (📞 410/850-7400), **National** (📞 410/859-8092), and **Thrifty** (📞 410/850-7112).

To reach Washington: Look for signs for I-195 and follow I-195 west until you see signs for Washington and the Baltimore-Washington Parkway (I-295); head south on

I-295. Get off I-295 when you see the signs for Route 50/New York Avenue, which leads into the District, via New York Avenue. Ask your hotel for specific directions from New York Avenue NE.

By Car

If you are like most visitors to Washington, you're planning to drive here via one of the following major highways: I-270, I-95, and I-295 from the north; I-95 and I-395, Route 1, and Route 301 from the south; Route 50/301 and Route 450 from the east; and Route 7, Route 50, I-66, and Route 29/211 from the west.

No matter which road you take, you will likely have to navigate part of the **Capital Beltway** (I-495 and I-95). The Beltway girds the city, about 66 miles (106km) around, with more than 56 interchanges or exits, and is nearly always congested, especially during weekday morning and evening rush hours (roughly 6–9:30am and 3–7pm). Commuter traffic on the Beltway rivals or surpasses that of L.A.'s major freeways, and drivers can get crazy, weaving in and out of traffic.

By Train

Amtrak (☎ 800/USA-RAIL; www. amtrak.com) offers daily service to Washington from New York, Boston, Chicago, and Los Angeles (you change trains in Chicago). Amtrak also travels daily from points south of Washington, including Raleigh, Charlotte, Atlanta, cities in Florida, and New Orleans.

Even faster, roomier, and more expensive are Amtrak's high-speed **Acela Express** trains. The trains travel 150 mph (242kmph), linking Boston, New York, and Washington.

Acela Express trains travel between New York and Washington in 2 hours and 50 minutes (about 20 min. faster than the Metroliner), and between Boston and Washington in about 6½ hours.

Amtrak trains arrive at historic **Union Station,** 50 Massachusetts Ave. NE (☎ 202/289-1908; www. unionstationdc.com).

By Bus

Coming from New York? **Bolt Bus** (www.boltbus.com) provides daily express service from Manhattan to Washington, and vice versa. Its buses are new, and outfitted with free wireless access and plug-ins for charging laptops and cell phones. The Bolt Bus picks up and drops off at Union Station. (A red Bolt Bus sign marks the spot.) Fares can range up to $34.

Another option is the well-known **Chinatown Bus** (www.china town-bus.com) that makes frequent runs between New York and Washington. Its buses are older and can be crowded, though. Fares range from $20 to $27.

Vamoose (☎ 301/718-0036; www.vamoosebus.com) offers service for $30 each way from New York City (near Penn Station) to Bethesda, MD, and Arlington, VA, where you can make a connection to D.C.'s Metro system.

Getting **Around**

By Metro

Metrorail's (www.wmta.com) system of 91 stations and six rail lines includes stops near most

sightseeing attractions and extends to suburban Maryland and northern Virginia. Six lines—Red, Blue, Orange, Yellow, Silver and

Green—connect at several points, making transfers easy. All but Yellow and Green Line trains stop at Metro Center; all except Red Line trains stop at L'Enfant Plaza; all but Blue, Silver, and Orange Line trains stop at Gallery Place/Chinatown.

Metro stations are identified by brown columns bearing the station's name topped by the letter M. Below the M is a colored stripe or stripes indicating the line or lines that stop there. The free *Metro System Pocket Guide* has a map and lists the closest Metro stops to points of interest. You can download a copy from www.wmata.com.

To enter or exit a Metro station, you need a computerized **SmarTrip card,** available at vending machines near the entrance. A SmarTrip card is a permanent, rechargeable card that must be used on MetroRail and bus now. No paper cards are accepted. The machines take credit cards or nickels, dimes, quarters, and bills from $1 to $20. At this time, the minimum fare to enter the system is $1.75, which pays for rides to and from any point within 7 miles (11km) of boarding during nonpeak hours; during peak hours (Mon–Fri 5–9:30am and 3–7pm), $2.15 takes you only 3 miles (5km). At press time, the maximum fare was $5.90. Metro Authority is always contemplating a fare hike, though.

If you plan to take several Metrorail trips during your stay, put more value on the SmarTrip card or reload the fare online. For stays of more than a few days, your best value is the **7-Day Fast Pass,** $59.25 per person for unlimited travel; **1-Day Rail Passes** cost $14.50 per person for unlimited passage that day, no time restrictions. You can buy these passes online now or use the passes/fare cards machine in the station. Giant, Safeway, and other grocery stores also sell fare cards.

Metrorail opens at 5am weekdays and 7am Saturday and Sunday, operating until midnight Sunday through Thursday, and until 3am Friday and Saturday. Call ☎ 202/637-7000, or visit www.wmata.com, for holiday hours and information on Metro routes.

By Bus

The **Metrobus** system operates 11,500 stops and 325 routes, extending into the Virginia and Maryland suburbs. Stops have red, white, and blue signs that tell you what buses pull into a stop, but not where they go. *Warning:* Don't rely on the bus schedules posted at bus stops—they're often out of date. For more information, call ☎ 202/637-7000.

Base fare in the District is $1.75 for those using cash or a SmarTrip; transfers are free and valid for 2 hours from boarding. If you'll be in Washington for a while and plan to use the buses a lot, consider a 7-day regional bus pass ($17.50) available online and at the Metro Center station and other outlets. Buy the pass at the Metro Center Sales Office, at 12th and F streets, the 12th Street entrance.

Most buses operate daily almost around the clock. Service is frequent on weekdays, especially during peak hours. On weekends and late at night, service is less frequent.

Up to two children age four and under ride free with a paying passenger on Metrobus. **Reduced fares** are available for seniors (☎ **202/637-7000**) and people with disabilities (☎ **202/962-2700**). If you leave something on a bus, a train, or in a station, call Lost and Found at ☎ **202/962-1195.**

By Car

More than half of all visitors arrive by car. Once you get here, though, my advice is to park it and walk or use the Metrorail. Traffic is always thick during the week, parking spots are scarce, and parking lots are pricey.

Watch out for **traffic circles.** Cars in the circle have the right of way, but no one heeds this rule. Cars zoom in without a glance at the cars already there.

Sections of certain streets become **one-way** at rush hour: Rock Creek Parkway, Canal Road, and 17th Street NW are three examples. Other streets during rush hour change the direction of some of their traffic lanes: Connecticut Avenue NW and 16th Street NW are the main ones. Lit-up traffic signs alert you to what's going on, but pay attention. You can make a right on a red light, unless a sign is posted prohibiting it.

Car Rentals/Shares

All the major car-rental companies are represented here. See area airports at the beginning of this chapter for phone numbers for each company's airport locations. Within the District, car-rental locations include **Avis,** 1722 M St. NW (☎ 202/467-6585) and 4400 Connecticut Ave. NW (☎ 202/686-5149); **Budget,** Union Station (☎ 202/289-5374); **Enterprise,** 1029 Vermont Ave. NW (☎ 202/393-0900); **Hertz,** Union Station (☎ 202/289-6084); and **Alamo,** Union Station (☎ 888/826-6893).

Whether you need a car for an hour or a month, **Zipcar** (☎ 866/494-7227; www.zipcar.com) offers its "members"—anyone can join for $25—flexible car-use arrangements, with gas, insurance, and other services included. Zipcar charges $8.25 an hour; its daily rate is $69. Given that hotels charge about $26 for overnight parking, the Zipcar deal, which includes

parking, could still be cost-effective.

Travelers with Limited Mobility

Washington, D.C., is one of the most accessible cities in the world for travelers with limited mobility. The best overall source of information about accessibility at specific Washington hotels, restaurants, shopping malls, and attractions is available from the nonprofit organization Access Information. You can read the information (including attractions) online at http://washington.org/DC-information/washington-dc-disability-information, or download a free copy of the ***Accessible Transportation Options Guide*** at www.wmata.com/accessibility/doc/Accessible_Transportation_Options.pdf.

The **Washington Metropolitan Transit Authority** also publishes accessibility information on its website **www.wmata.com**, or you can call ☎ **202/962-1100** with questions about Metro services for travelers with disabilities, including how to obtain an ID card that entitles you to discounted fares. For up-to-date information about how Metro is running the day you're using it, call ☎ **202/962-1212.**

Each station has an elevator with Braille number plates and wide fare gates for wheelchair users; rail cars are fully accessible. Metro has installed punctuated rubber tiles to warn visually impaired riders that they're nearing the tracks; barriers between rail cars prevent the blind from mistaking the gap for entry to a car. For the hearing impaired, flashing lights indicate arriving trains; for the visually impaired, door chimes let you know when doors are closing. Train operators make station and on-board announcements of train destinations and stops. Nearly all

Metrobuses have wheelchair lifts and kneel at the curb. The TTY number for Metro information is ☎ 202/962-2033.

Major Washington museums, including all **Smithsonian museum buildings,** are accessible to wheelchair visitors. A comprehensive free publication called *Smithsonian Accessibility Program* lists all services available to visitors with mobility issues. Call ☎ **202/633-2921** or TTY 202/633-4353, or find the information online at www.si.edu/Visit/VisitorsWithDisabilities.

Likewise, theaters and all of the memorials are equipped to accommodate visitors with disabilities. There's limited parking for visitors with disabilities at some of these locations. Call ahead for accessibility information and special services.

Fast **Facts**

AREA CODES In the District of Columbia, it's ☎ 202; in suburban Virginia, ☎ 703; in suburban Maryland, ☎ 301. You must use the area code when dialing any number, even local calls within the District or to nearby Maryland or Virginia suburbs.

ATMS Automated teller machines (ATMs) are on most every block. Most accept Visa, MasterCard, American Express, and ATM cards from other U.S. banks. Expect to pay up to $3 per transaction if you're not using your own bank's ATM.

BUSINESS HOURS Offices are usually open weekdays from 9am to 5pm. Banks are open Monday through Thursday from 9am to 3pm, 9am to 5pm on Friday, and sometimes Saturday mornings. Stores typically open between 9 and 10am and close between 5 and 6pm from Monday through Saturday. Stores in shopping complexes or malls tend to stay open late: until about 9pm on weekdays and weekends, and many malls and larger department stores are open on Sundays.

CAR RENTALS See "Getting Around," earlier in this chapter.

DRUGSTORES **CVS,** Washington's major drugstore chain (with more than 40 stores), has two convenient 24-hour locations: in the West End, at 2240 M St. NW (☎ **202/296-9876**), and at Dupont Circle (☎ **202/785-1466**), with a round-the-clock pharmacy.

ELECTRICITY Like Canada, the United States uses 110 to 120 volts AC (60 cycles), compared to 220 to 240 volts AC (50 cycles) in most of Europe, Australia, and New Zealand. If your small appliances use 220 to 240 volts, you'll need a 110-volt transformer and a plug adapter with two flat parallel pins to operate them here. Downward converters that change 220 to 240 volts to 110 to 120 volts are difficult to find in the United States, so bring one with you.

EMBASSIES & CONSULATES All embassies are in D.C., the nation's capital. Online, you will find a complete listing, with links to each embassy, at www.embassy.org/embassies/index.html.

Here are the addresses of several: **Australia,** 1601 Massachusetts Ave. NW (☎ 202/797-3000; www.usa.embassy.gov.au); **Canada,** 501 Pennsylvania Ave. NW (☎ 202/682-1740; www.canadianembassy.org); **Ireland,** 2234 Massachusetts Ave. NW (☎ 202/462-3939; www.embassyofireland.org); **New**

Zealand, 37 Observatory Circle NW (☎ 202/328-4800; www.nzembassy. org/usa); and the **United Kingdom,** 3100 Massachusetts Ave. NW (☎ 202/588-6500; http://ukinusa. fco.gov.uk/en).

EMERGENCIES In any emergency, call ☎ **911.**

HOLIDAYS Banks, government offices, post offices, and many stores, restaurants, and museums are closed on the following legal national holidays: January 1 (New Year's Day), the third Monday in January (Martin Luther King, Jr., Day), January 20 (Inauguration Day), the third Monday in February (Presidents' Day, Washington's Birthday), the last Monday in May (Memorial Day), July 4 (Independence Day), the first Monday in September (Labor Day), the second Monday in October (Columbus Day), November 11 (Veterans' Day/Armistice Day), the fourth Thursday in November (Thanksgiving Day), and December 25 (Christmas).

HOSPITALS If you don't require immediate ambulance transportation but still need emergency-room treatment, call one of the following hospitals (and get directions): **Children's National Medical Center,** 111 Michigan Ave. NW (☎ 888/884-2327); **George Washington University Hospital,** 900 23rd St. NW at Washington Circle (☎ 202/715-4000); **MedStar Georgetown University Hospital,** 3800 Reservoir Rd. NW (☎ 202/444-2000); or **Howard University Hospital,** 2042 Georgia Ave. NW (☎ 202/865-6100).

INTERNET ACCESS Your hotel is your best bet since many hotels now offer free Internet access. **Tryst,** 2459 18th St., NW, (☎ **202/232-5500**) and **Busboys and Poets,** 2021 14th St., NW, (☎ **202/387-7638**) are also good stops for free wireless access. Most

Starbucks and **Peet's Coffees** also offer free Internet access.

LIQUOR LAWS The legal age for purchase and consumption of alcoholic beverages is 21; proof of age is required, so bring an ID when you go out.

Do not carry open containers of alcohol in your car or any public area that isn't zoned for alcohol consumption. The police can fine you on the spot. And nothing will ruin your trip faster than getting a citation for DUI (driving under the influence), so don't even think about driving while intoxicated.

MAIL The main post office in the capital is the **National Capitol Station,** 2 Massachusetts Ave. NE (☎ **202/636-1259;** www.usps. com). Mailboxes are blue with a red-and-white stripe and carry the inscription U.S. MAIL. All U.S. addresses have a five-digit postal code (or zip code), after the two-letter state abbreviation. This code is essential for prompt delivery.

At press time, domestic postage rates were 35¢ for a postcard and 49¢ for a letter. For international mail, a first-class letter of up to 1 ounce costs $1.20. A first-class international postcard also costs $1.20.

NEWSPAPERS & MAGAZINES Washington has two daily newspapers: the *Washington Post* (www.washingtonpost.com) and the *Washington Times* (www.washingtontimes. com). The Friday "Weekend" section of the *Post* is essential for finding out what's going on, recreation-wise. *City Paper,* published every Thursday and available free at downtown shops and restaurants, covers some of the same material but is a better guide to the club and art-gallery scene.

Also on newsstands is *Washingtonian,* a monthly magazine with features, often about the "100

Best" this or that (doctors, restaurants, and so on) in Washington; the magazine also offers a calendar of events, restaurant reviews, and profiles of Washingtonians.

POLICE In an emergency, dial ☎ **911.** For a nonemergency, call ☎ **202/727-4404.**

SAFETY Washington, like any urban area, has a criminal element, so it's important to stay alert and take normal safety precautions.

Ask your hotel front-desk staff or the city's tourist office if you're in doubt about which neighborhoods are safe.

SMOKING In 2006, D.C. lawmakers banned smoking in bars, restaurants, and public places, with exemptions for outdoor areas, hotel rooms, retail tobacco outlets, and cigar bars.

TAXES The U.S. has no value-added tax (VAT) or other indirect tax at the national level. The sales tax on merchandise is 5.75% in D.C. The tax on restaurant meals is 10%, and you'll pay 14.5% hotel tax. The hotel tax in Maryland varies by county from 5% to 8%. The hotel tax in Virginia also varies by county, averaging about 9.75%.

TELEPHONE & FAX Private corporations run the telephone system in the U.S., so rates—especially for long-distance service and operator-assisted calls—can vary widely. Generally, hotel surcharges on long-distance and local calls are astronomical, so you're usually better off using a **cell phone.**

Many convenience groceries and packaging services sell **prepaid calling cards** in denominations up to $50; these can be the least expensive way to call home. Many public phones at airports now accept American Express, MasterCard, and Visa credit cards. You may want to look into leasing a cellphone for the duration of your trip.

Most long-distance and international calls can be dialed directly from any phone. **For calls within the United States and to Canada,** dial 1 followed by the area code and the seven-digit number. **For other international calls,** dial 011 followed by the country code, city code, and the telephone number of the person you are calling.

Calls to area codes **800, 888, 877,** and **866** are toll free. However, calls to numbers in area codes **700** and **900** (chat lines, bulletin boards, "dating" services, and so on) can be very expensive—usually a charge of 95¢ to $3 or more per minute, and they sometimes have minimum charges that can run as high as $15 or more.

For **reversed-charge or collect calls,** and for person-to-person calls, dial zero, followed by the area code and number you want; an operator will then come on the line to assist you. If you're calling abroad, ask for the overseas operator.

For **local directory assistance (information),** dial ☎ 411; for long-distance information, dial ☎ 1, then the appropriate area code and 555-1212.

TIME Washington D.C. observes Eastern Standard Time (EST), like New York City. **Daylight saving time** is in effect from 2am on the second Sunday in March through 2am on the first Sunday in November, except in most of Arizona, Hawaii, and Puerto Rico. Daylight saving time moves the clock 1 hour ahead of standard time. At 1am on the first Sunday in November, clocks are set back 1 hour.

TIPPING In hotels, tip **bellhops** at least $1 per bag, and tip the **chamber staff** $1 to $2 per day. Tip the **doorman** or **concierge** only if he or she has provided you with some specific service (for example, calling a cab for you or obtaining difficult-to-get theater tickets). Tip the **valet-parking attendant** $1 every time you get your car.

In restaurants, bars, and night-clubs, tip **service staff** 15% to 20% of the check, tip **bartenders** 10% to 15%, tip **checkroom attendants** $1 per garment, and tip **valet-parking attendants** $1 per vehicle. Tipping is not expected in cafeterias and fast-food restaurants.

Tip **cab drivers** 15% of the fare.

As for other service personnel, tip **skycaps** at airports at least $1 per bag, and tip **hairdressers** and **barbers** 15% to 20%.

Tipping ushers at movies and theaters, and gas-station attendants, is not expected.

TOILETS You won't find public toilets or "restrooms" on the streets in D.C., but they can be found in hotel lobbies, bars, restaurants, coffee shops, museums, department stores, railway and bus stations, and service stations. Large hotels and fast-food restaurants are probably the best bet for good, clean facilities. Restaurants and bars in heavily visited areas may reserve their restrooms for patrons; purchasing a cup of coffee or soft drink will usually qualify you as a customer.

WEATHER Visit www.weather.com. Also see the chart on p 171. ●

Index

See also Accommodations and Restaurant indexes, below.

A

Accessible transportation, 176–177
Accommodations, 162–168. *See also* Accommodations Index
Acela Express trains, 174
Adams Morgan, 78–79
Adamson Gallery, 106
African American Civil War Memorial and Museum, 83
Air travel, 171–174
Amtrak, 173, 174
Antique Row, 22, 109–110
Area codes, 177, 179
Arena Stage, 157
Arlington House, 23
Arlington National Cemetery, 23
Art galleries, 106
Arts and entertainment, 156–158
Atlas Performing Arts Center, 157
ATMs (automated teller machines), 177

B

Baltimore-Washington International Airport, 173
Barracks Row, 99
Barrel, 24, 152
Bars, 24
Bartholdi Park, 98
Bell, Alexander Graham, residence, 33
Betsy Fisher, 87, 106–107
Biking, 121
Blue Mercury, 86–87
Blues Alley, 149–150
Bohemian Caverns, 150
Bolt Bus, 174
Bookstores, 106
Booth, John Wilkes, 5
Buffalo Exchange, 81–82
Business hours, 177
Bus tours, 10
Bus travel, 174, 175

C

Cady's Alley, 90, 110–111
Café Saint-Ex, 148–149
Canoeing, 117, 120
Capital Bikeshare, 121

Capitol Building, 12, 17, 28, 36
Capitol Hill, 96–100
Capitol Hill Books, 99, 106
Capitol Visitors Center, 12
Carling Nichols, 110
Car rentals, 172, 173, 176
Carter Barron Amphitheater, 117
Car travel, 174, 175–176
Cherry Blossom Festival, 6, 126
Cherry blossoms, 6
Chinatown Bus, 174
C&O Canal, 91, 119–121
C&O Canal Towpath, 47, 119, 120
Consulates, 177–178
Cultural Tourism D.C., 52, 170
Curator's Office, 106
Cusp, 107

D

The Dandelion Patch, 109
DAR Constitution Hall, 157
Dawn Price Baby, 106
D.C. Circulator, 146
D.C. Tours, 10
DC Improv, 157
Dean & Deluca, 109
Destination D.C., 170
Disabilities, travelers with, 176–177
District of Columbia Arts Center, 79
Dollar, 173
Douglass, Frederick, 54
Drugstores, 177
Dumbarton House, 33
Dumbarton Oaks, 22, 122
Dupont Circle, 84–87
Dupont Memorial Fountain, 86

E

Eastern Market, 5, 16, 99–100, 112
Electricity, 177
Ella-Rue, 89
Embassies, 177–178
Embassy Row, 41
Emergencies, 178
Evermay, 88

F

FDR Memorial, 11
Federal Bureau of Investigation (FBI), 29–30
Federal Reserve Building, 12
Fine Art, 106
Folger Shakespeare Library, 37–38, 98

Folger Theatre, 157
Food trucks, 141
Ford's Theatre, 5, 53, 157
Ford's Theatre National Historic Site, 93
Fort DeRussey, 116
14th Street/U Street Corridor, 80–83
Foxhall House, 33
Frederick Douglass National Historic Site, 54
Friendship Heights, 109

G

The Galleries on 14th Street, 81, 106
Gays and lesbian nightlife, 148
Georgetown, 6, 9, 88–91
getting to, 91
outdoor activities, 122–123
Georgetown Flea Market, 112
Georgetown Running Co., 107
Georgetown University, 90
Gravelly Point, 47
Gray Line Buses, 10
Great Ape House, 46
Greater U Street Heritage Trail, 82
Great Falls, 120–121

H

Hemphill Fine Arts, 106
Hilton Washington, 50
Holidays, 178
Home Rule, 81, 110
Hospitals, 178
Hotels, 162–168. *See also* Accommodations Index
House gallery, 29
Howard University, 83
Hu's Shoes, 112

I

Independence Day (July 4th), 170
Intermix, 107
International Spy Museum, 29, 45, 94–95
Internet access, 178

J

Jefferson Building of the Library of Congress, 37
Jefferson Memorial, 11–12
July 4th (Independence Day), 170

K

Kayaking, 120
Kennedy, Jackie house, 33
Kennedy, John F.
  residences, 33, 50
  gravesite, 23
Kennedy Center for the Performing Arts, 158
Kerry, John, residence, 33
Kids
  restaurants, 134
  shopping, 106
  Washington for, 44–47
Kids' Farm, 46
King, Martin Luther, Jr., 11
Kissinger, Henry, former home, 33
Korean War Veterans Memorial, 11
Kramerbooks & Afterwords Café, 21, 84

L

L'Enfant, Pierre, 23, 36
L'Enfant's Grid, 36
Library of Congress, 16–17, 54
Lincoln, Abraham, 5, 9, 54, 86
  Cottage, 56
Lincoln Memorial, 9
Lincoln Museum, 53
Lincoln Theatre, 82, 158
Liquor laws, 178
Lou Lou, 86, 108
Lover's Lane, 122–123

M

Madame Tussauds, 92
Mail, 178
The Mall, 18, 125–126
Map of the Political Stars, 31–33
Marian Koshland Science Museum, 94
Martin Luther King, Jr. Memorial, 11
Martin's Tavern, 56, 151
Marvin, 149
Metro, weekend hours, 146
Metrobus, 175
Metro Mutts, 111
Metrorail (Metro), 174–175
Middle C Music, 111
Miss Lydia English's Georgetown Female Seminary, 33
Miss Pixie's, 81, 110
Montrose Park, 89
Mount Vernon Estate and Gardens, 55

Mount Vernon Trail, 123
M Street, corner of Wisconsin Avenue and, 23
Muzette, 149

N

National Air and Space Museum, 45
The National Archives, 16, 30
The National Building Museum, 40, 44, 94
National Cathedral, 21–22, 41
The National Gallery of Art, 6, 12, 39–40
National Geographic Explorer's Hall, 87
National Museum of African American History and Culture, 38
National Museum of American History, 4–5, 13
National Museum of Natural History, 44–45
National Museum of the American Indian, 39
National Museum of Women in the Arts, 92
National Park Service website, 170
National Portrait Gallery, 40, 53
National Theatre, 158
National World War II Memorial, 10
National Zoo, 5, 15, 46
Nature Center, Rock Creek Park Planetarium and, 115
Newspapers and magazines, 178
Nightlife, 146–152
Nine West, 108

O

Oak Hill Cemetery, 88–89, 123
Octagon Museum, 51
Off the Record Bar, 4, 13, 24, 146, 151
The Old Print Gallery, 111
Old Stone House, 91
Olmsted Walk, 46

P

Paddle boats, 126
Pearson's, 109
Penn Quarter, 92–95
The Pentagon, 32
Pets, 111–112
Phillips Collection, 85
Picnics, Rock Creek Park, 116

Planetarium and Nature Center, Rock Creek Park, 115
Police, 179
Politics and Prose, 106
Potomac River, 125
President Lincoln's Cottage, 56
Proof, 95, 152
Proper Topper, 108

R

Rainfall, average, 171
Redeem, 108
Reflecting Pool, 125
Restaurants. See also Restaurants Index
  best bets, 132
  food trucks, 141
  for kids, 134
  reservations, 138
  seating at the bar, 138
Rock Creek Horse Center, 116
Rock Creek Park, 115–116
The Rock Creek Park Planetarium and Nature Center, 115
Rock Creek Park Tennis Center, 116–117
Ronald Reagan Washington National Airport, 172
Room & Board, 111
Roosevelt, Franklin, 11
R Street in Georgetown, 22

S

Safety, 179
Sara's Market, 123
Seasons, 170
Senate gallery, 29
Sequoia, 24
Severgnini, Beppe, 36
Sewall-Belmont House & Museum, 53–54, 97–98
The Shakespeare Theatre, 19, 95
Shakespeare Theatre Company, 158
Shoes, 112
Shopping, best bets, 102
Shuttles, 172
Smithsonian Castle, 38–39
The Smithsonian Information Center, 170
Smoking, 179
Spring, 170
The Star-Spangled Banner, 51–52
Studio Theatre, 158
Sullivan's Toy Store, 106
The Supreme Court, 18, 29

T

Taxes, 179
Taxis, 171
Taylor, Elizabeth, home, 33
Teddy and the Bully Bar, 87
Telephone, 179
Temperature, average, 171
Tennis Center, Rock Creek Park, 116–117
Theater J, 158
Theodore Roosevelt Island Park, 117
Thomas Pink, 108
Tidal Basin, 5, 12, 44, 125, 126
Time zones, 179
Timothy Paul Carpets & Textiles, 111
Tiny Jewel Box, 111
Tipping, 179–180
Toilets, 180
Tomb of the Unknowns, 23
Tourist offices, 170
Train travel, 174
Tudor Place, 33, 89
Tugooh Toys, 106

U

Ultra Violet Flowers, 109
Union Station, 40, 96–97
U.S. Capitol Building, 12, 17, 28, 36

V

Vamoose, 174
Verizon Center, 95
Vietnam Veterans Memorial, 9–10
Violet Boutique, 79, 109

W

Walking tours, self-guided, 52
Warner Theatre, 158
Washington, D.C., Visitor Information Center, 170
Washington, George, Mount Vernon Estate and Gardens, 55
Washington Dulles International Airport, 172–173
Washingtonian, 178–179
Washington Monument, 10, 38, 51
Washington National Cathedral, 21–22, 41
Washington Navy Yard Museum, 100
Washington Post, 178
Washington Times, 178
Weather, 180
Websites, 170

The White House, 12, 30–31
Willard InterContinental, 52
Wisconsin Avenue and M Street, 23
Wolf Trap Foundation for the Performing Arts, 158
Woodrow Wilson House, 50, 85
Woolly Mammoth Theatre Company, 158

Z

Zipcar, 176

Accommodations

The Capella, 163
The Carlyle, 163
The Dupont Circle, 163
The Embassy Row Hotel, 163
The Fairmont Washington, 163–164
Four Seasons Georgetown, 164
Georgetown Inn, 164
Glover Park Hotel, 164
Hay-Adams, 164–165
Hotel George, 165
Hotel Monaco, 165
Hotel Palomar, 165
Hotel Rouge, 165
The Jefferson Hotel, 166
The Madison Hotel, 166
Mandarin Oriental, 166
Marriott Marquis, 166
Mason and Rook, 166
The Mayflower, 167
Ritz-Carlton Georgetown, 167
The River Inn, 167
St. Regis Hotel, 167
The Tabard Inn, 165
Topaz Hotel, 167–168
Washington Plaza Hotel, 168
W Hotel, 168
Willard InterContinental Hotel, 168

Restaurants

Acadiana, 133
Amys, 47
Beefsteak, 133
Ben's Chili Bowl, 82–83, 133
Black Salt, 133
BLT Steak, 31, 133
Blue Duck Tavern, 133–134
Bourbon, 134
Bourbon Steak, 91
Brasserie Beck, 134
Busboys & Poets, 134
Cafe Deluxe, 134–135
Café Deluxe, 22, 134
Café Milano, 135

Café Saint-Ex, 135
Capital Grille, 135
The Capital Grille, 24
Center Café, 40
Central Michel Richard, 135
Charlie Palmer Steak, 24
Chef Geoff's, 134
Chez Billy, 136
Circa, 86
Comet Ping Pong, 134
Commissary DC, 80
Daily Grill, 136
The Diner, 79
District Chophouse and Brewery, 45
Estadio, 136
Filomena Ristorante, 136
Fiola Mare, 136–137
Floriana Restaurant, 137
Founding Farmers, 137
Georgia Brown's, 137
Great Falls Tavern, 120
The Hamilton, 137–138
Indique, 138
Jaleo, 138
Johnny's Half Shell, 138
Kellari, 139
Komi, 139
Kramerbooks & Afterwords Café, 84
Lauriol Plaza, 139
Le Diplomate, 139
Leopold's Kafe Konditorei, 90–91
Mane Grill, 16, 46
Masseria, 139
Matchbox, 93
Medium Rare, 139
Momofuku/Milk Bar, 139–140
The Monocle, 24
Occidental, 52
Old Anglers Inn, 120
Paul, 12, 126
Pearl Dive Oyster Palace, 140
Perry's, 140
Proof, 95, 140
Provision, 140
Range, 140–141
Restaurant Nora, 141
The Riggsby, 141
Rose's Luxury, 141–142
1789, 141
Smith Point, 24
Sonoma Restaurant and Wine Bar, 142
The Source, 13, 142
Teaism, 142
Teddy and the Bully Bar, 87
Ted's Bulletin, 99, 142
Tryst, 78
Tune Inn, 24
Zaytinya, 142

Photo **Credits**